DALE ... an illustrated History

Acknowledgements, Map of Dale	2
Foreword by Mrs O Lloyd-Philipps	3
Ladies of Dale c1900	4

EARLY HISTORY:

Prehistoric finds	5
Roman, Early Medieval, Viking raids	7
The de Vale Family	9
Henry Tudor	10

SEAFARING:

16th and 17th Century	14
Pirates and smugglers	15
Lighthouse	16
Coastal trading	18
Limekilns	20
Boat building	21
Fishing	22
Disasters	24
The Coastguards	26

FARMS and FARMING:

Work on the farm	29
The Windmill	32
Castle Estate and farmhouses	33
Allenbrook and Dale Nurseries	36

Dale Castle	3
Older houses in Dale	4

MILITARY PRESENCE:

West Blockhouse	43
Dale Fort	46
Flying Machine	49
World War 1, War Memorial	50
World War 2 and beyond	56

FAITH and EDUCATION:

St James' Church	63
Chapels	66
The School	68

WORK and LEISURE:

Occupations, The Post	72
Services	78
Village Hall	79
Dale Fair and Carnival	81
Stormy Weather	84
Yachting Adventures and Yacht Club	86
Fun and Fame	89
Pubs, Clubs and Organisations	90
Final Thoughts	95
Select Sources and Bibliography	96

FOREWORD by Mrs Osra Lloyd-Philipps

I am most grateful to the Dale Women's Institute for the opportunity to write a few words as an introduction to this interesting book on Dale.

I came to live in Dale in 1957, when I married my late husband, Hugh. My maternal grandmother was an Allen and my father, Colonel Linton, was a serving soldier. I soon settled into life at Dale Castle with the extended family around me. It was a happy and busy home, and it was from here that the Estate was run with the upkeep of the agricultural land and farmsteads our primary concern. My mother-in-law, Margaret (Marjory) Lloyd-Philipps, was a founder member of the Dale WI and took an active part in village life for many years. During his life, my husband always tried to maintain the character of Dale and to conserve its heritage. As a result, Dale is relatively unspoilt. It has changed only gradually over the years which is, perhaps, one of the reasons why it holds such an important place in the hearts of so many.

I am very pleased that ladies of the Dale Women's Institute have written this first illustrated history of such a delightful, coastal village. The book reflects many aspects of Dale's past, both the mundane and the colourful, and it has been carefully and diligently researched. I commend it to all those who love Dale.

Mr and Mrs HVB Lloyd-Philipps receive, on the occasion of their marriage, a gift from Mr John Davies on behalf of the tenants of Dale Castle Estate

Osra Lloyd-Philipps
Dale Castle
May 2000

LADIES OF DALE c.1900

left to right: Miss Cilla Evans, Mrs Ellen Corrigan

ACKNOWLEDGEMENTS

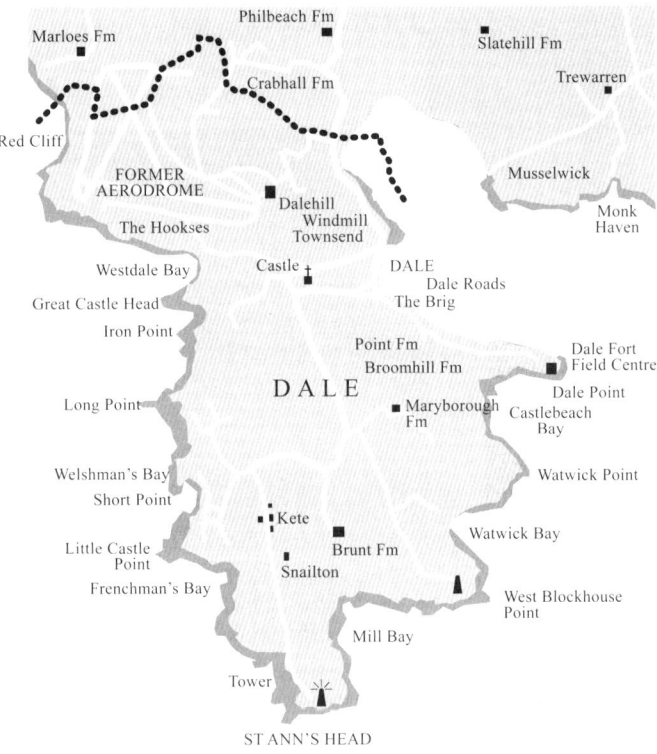

THE DALE PENINSULA

Skokholm Island is in the Parish

Those who assisted the Dale Women's Institute Project Group with information, photographs, etc to enable us to compile this book are too numerous to mention individually. Without such overwhelming support the task would have been very difficult and much less enjoyable. Our grateful thanks to each and everyone involved. Our thanks also to the Heritage Lottery Fund who kindly provided a grant to cover the majority costs of the Project.

The book is Dale W I's response to the 'Pathway to the 21st Century' initiative by the National Federation of W I's, Wales.

The Project Group accepts responsibility for any errors and omissions.

DALE ... an illustrated History
Copyright © 2000 Dale Women's Institute
All rights reserved. No part of this publication may be reproduced, stored in a retrieval system, or transmitted in any form or by any means, without the permission of Dale Women's Institute.

ISBN 0-9538693-0-X

Published by Dale Women's Institute of Dale, Pembrokeshire.
Printed by CIT brace harvatt, Haverfordwest

Early History

PREHISTORIC FINDS

The earliest traces of human activity in Dale probably date back to the Mesolithic or Middle Stone Age (10-6,000 BC). Tiny flints and other stone tools typical of this period have been found at clifftop sites mainly on the western side of the Dale peninsula. It is thought that these areas were used intermittently for flint working by nomadic groups. Flint pebbles were probably found on the beach as they still are today. Buried flakes of flint and crude implements provide clues to these early hunters.

During the next 2000 years slow changes in people's lifestyle took place in the British Isles. In some parts coastal sites were more permanently occupied with shellfish forming an important part of the inhabitants' diet. This may have happened in Dale as several stone implements interpreted by some archaeologists as 'limpet or shellfish scoops' have been found.

An even more radical change occurred after 3,500 BC when farming became the normal way of obtaining food, pottery was made and huts built as living accommodation. However, tools and weapons were still made from stone and flint and the period is known as the New Stone Age! Some beautifully polished axes and other flint and stone implements have been found on several inland sites in the Dale area – Brunt, Snailton and Hooks' farms.

A few Bronze Age remains have been recorded from Dale – a bronze ring possibly from Great Castle Head, a barbed and tanged flint arrowhead from Short Point. A possible standing stone at Brunt Farm has now been ploughed in.

Many of the above sites were recorded in the Archaeological Survey of Pembrokeshire 1896-1907. The Dale area was surveyed by Mr Henry Mathias who himself collected and unearthed many of the stones and flints. Henry Mathias was related to both the Lloyd-Philipps and Rind families of Dale. He had been a Solicitor in Haverfordwest but after his retirement he became known as a dedicated amateur archaeologist. Mr Mathias presented some of his finds to Tenby Museum where they can still be seen today. The Survey recorded that a shaft existed near Little Castle Head which was reputedly an ancient copper mine but it was filled in about 1850 after a horse had fallen down it!

Examples of worked flints from the Dale area – actual size

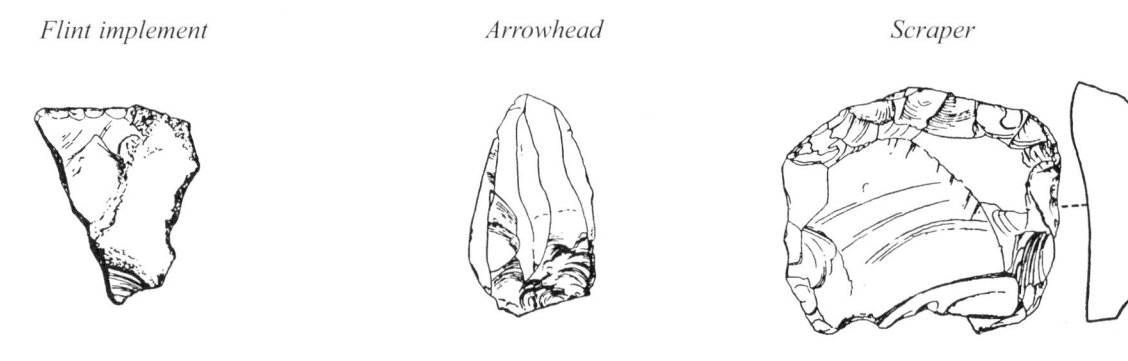

| Flint implement | Arrowhead | Scraper |

found to the west of Kete   *found at Short Point*   *found at Snailton*

More archaeological work was done both by Professor Grimes and the Dyfed Archaeological Trust at Dale Point and it was discovered that a late Bronze Age site existed there with pottery and beaker finds. The Dale Point site has a massive mound and ditch with evidence of fortifications of a date before 790 BC – radio-carbon dating tests were used to verify this. No other promontory forts in Pembrokeshire have produced readings of such an early date.

An even bigger fortification exists at Great Castle Head. The banks and ditches of these promontory forts, which are still visible today, are typical of the Iron Age (from 600 BC). The inhabitants would have felt quite secure in their clifftop settlement with ramparts and doors to protect them from attackers seeking slaves and cattle. Few 'iron' artefacts have been found but pottery and stone spindle whorls (small stone weights used for hand-spinning) have been excavated from the two larger promontory forts which probably continued to be used throughout the years when the Romans were occupying England and parts of Wales.

ROMAN PERIOD

During the first century AD, Dale was part of the territory of the Demetae tribe. It seems that this tribe was not troublesome to the Roman army. Possibly the Roman fleet with one of its bases at Cardiff had control over the Severn and Irish seas and the coastal inhabitants of the Demetae lands welcomed them. Certainly the coastline of Pembrokeshire was mapped by geographers of the Roman period – on one map what looks like St Ann's Head is named Octapitatum Promontory. It seems quite likely that Romano-British traders visited the Dale peninsula in their journeys by sea from Carmarthen and even England as pottery remains have been found at several promontory forts, including the two main ones in Dale. Many Roman coins have been found in Pembrokeshire suggesting that trade was well established. We know that seal skins were among British exports – maybe they came from this area.

In about 250 AD the Roman Empire was weakened by internal struggles and records show that Irish pirates among others were making raids on British boundaries. Irish invaders or traders almost made this part of Pembrokeshire 'Little Ireland'. After the withdrawal of the Roman fleet towards the end of the fourth century, Irish raids intensified, one of the main objects being to capture slaves. Undoubtedly, the promontory forts in Dale would be needed as strongholds if these raiders were seen approaching.

EARLY MEDIEVAL PERIOD (400-1100 AD)

Little is known of Dale during the next few hundred years.

Christianity was introduced at some point with nearby Celtic churches at St Ishmaels and St Brides. There was plenty of recorded movement along the West Wales seaways by early monks who travelled to and from Ireland, Scotland, Brittany and Wales, spreading the doctrines of Christianity.

An excavated settlement on Gateholm, less than an hour's walk from Dale, has been dated to this period.

VIKING RAIDS

Between the 9th and 11th centuries Viking warriors swept down on the Celtic settlements of Pembrokeshire and other parts of Wales. It was from their kingdom around Dublin that these ferocious heathen raiders set sail across to West Wales attracted by the rich treasures of places like St Davids which was frequently sacked and burned.

Dale is a Scandinavian word meaning 'valley'. Other local place names such as Skalmey (the old name for Skomer), Skokholm, Musselwick and Hasguard are also of Norse origin. The Vikings may even have settled here on a more permanent basis. At any rate we can conclude that they knew our village well enough to give it their own name.

THE DE VALE FAMILY

By the year 1100 much of Pembrokeshire was under Norman control with castles built at strategic points and the land taken over by Anglo-Norman settlers. The son of one of these may have been Hubert de Vale who was a witness to a charter at St Dogmaels in 1131. De Vale was probably the Latin translation of the Norse 'Dalr' meaning valley. This may be the earliest written evidence that Dale was now under Anglo-Norman control.

Nothing is known about the arrival of the de Vales in the area. They may have come from Devon with an Anglo-Norman adventurer. The de Vales held their land from the Lords of Walwyn's Castle, part of the Earldom of Pembroke.

Robert Fitz Richard de Vale is said to have joined Strongbow's invasion of Ireland in 1170. He acquired land there and gave some of this to found a nunnery in Co Kildare in 1200.

During the unrest of the early years of the thirteenth century and possibly before, danger from Welsh rebels may have threatened even the Dale area. A recent excavation of Great Castle Head has produced pottery remains of this period, suggesting that the inhabitants may have been panicked into re-occupying the Iron Age fortress.

Gilbert de Vale was now the land-holder of Dale. He held the office of Seneschal (Steward) at Pembroke around 1240, as well as being an important land-holder. He had been granted land and a mill at St Ishmaels and the stream of Corslery to make a fishery for eels! More charters were witnessed by him and other land agreements made.

The manor of Dale seemed to be a growing village during the continuing peace of the thirteenth century. Robert de Vale, the next lord of the manor, appears as quite an influential personality. He witnessed several charters in the Court of Pembroke and bought land in North Pembrokeshire. Perhaps Robert's most high-powered achievement was the granting of a Royal Charter on 5th December 1293 to hold a weekly market and annual fair lasting three days in his manor of Dale on the Feast of the Exaltation of the Holy Cross.

Robert died in 1297. He had no male heir to succeed and his lands were partitioned between his daughters and their husbands. Their descendants succeeded to the lordship of the Manor.

HENRY TUDOR

Henry Tudor chose Milford Haven to land his invasion force of 2000 men when making his bid to remove Richard III from the English throne. Henry, who had been born at Pembroke Castle, had been forced to spend several years in exile in France.

It seems generally agreed that Mill Bay was the first landing place on 7th August 1485. Henry came ashore at dusk and luckily the weather was fine. He is supposed to have commented "This place is Brunt" meaning steep or possibly meaning that its name was Brunt. The landing party may have been a small advanced detachment. When it was seen that there was no opposition, the other ships, who may have been approaching under cover of darkness, could have landed in safety. By landing on the north bank of the Haven, Henry could bypass Pembroke Castle which was held by Richard's constable.

What reception was waiting for him at Dale is uncertain but there are no accounts of an armed struggle. A version of events is given by a biographer of Rhys ap Thomas, the Welsh magnate who fortunately turned out to be Henry's ally. According to this version, which may be rather embroidered, Rhys, who had sworn an oath

Henry Tudor marching to Dale

that Richard's enemies would never land on the shores of Milford Haven "except over my bellie", was having second thoughts about supporting Richard especially as Henry seemed to be getting more popular! Rhys consulted his bard and prophet, Robert of Dale – no further details of this enigmatic poet are given – as to whether Henry was likely to be successful. Robert replied in verse –

> *Full well I wend*
> *That in the end*
> *Richmond sprung from British race*
> *From out this land the boar shall chace.*

Henry's title, inherited from his father, was the Earl of Richmond. The boar was a reference to Richard whose banner portrayed this beast. Rhys himself was sometimes referred to as the Raven and Henry as the Dragon for the same reason. Early bards had prophesied that one day the Red Dragon would return in triumph to avenge the English conquest of Wales.

Rhys also asked his prophet whether Henry would land at Milford Haven and the reply was –

> *Hie thee to the dale*
> *I'll to the vale*
> *To drink good ale*
> *And so I pre, han a care of us all.*

Rhys then mustered his force at his Castle of Carew, mounted his 'goodlie courser' Llwyd Baxe or Grey Fetterlocks and set forth in the most martial manner towards Dale and, there meeting the Earle of Richmond, made humble tender of his service and laying him down on the ground *"suffered the Earle to pass over him; soe to make good his promise to King Richard"* that *"no one should enter in at Milford onlesse he came first over my bellie"*. The writer goes on to say that local tradition says Rhys went under the arch of a small bridge called Mullock Bridge and there remained till Henry had crossed it.

John Barrett as one of Henry Tudor's entourage

At Dale a noble and stirring speech was made by Henry and he was well received by the Welshmen who were – *transported with his eloquence, some kissing his hands, some his feete... then beating up their drums, sounding their trumpets, fell to shouts and acclamations and crying to heaven "King Henrie, King Henrie. Down with the bragging White Boar"*. This was followed by an equally stirring speech from Rhys in which he urged Henry to call his French forces ashore and lose no time in starting his advance to England.

The Bishop of St Davids then gave a sermon. Henry and Rhys decided on a campaign plan with Henry taking the route northwards through Cardigan and Rhys guarding his flank with a more easterly route through Carmarthen. They would meet again at Shrewsbury. Unfortunately this account, which was written in the early seventeenth century seems to be more concerned with boosting Rhys's reputation than historical accuracy; therefore much of it has to be taken as legend.

However, another manuscript states that Henry did indeed spend the night at Dale where he knighted eight of his supporters and at dawn the next day set out for Haverfordwest. He moved swiftly through Wales without encountering any opposition to speak of, met up with Rhys ap Thomas and other leaders who brought reinforcements and on 22nd August triumphed at Bosworth.

RE-ENACTMENT

On August 7 1985, a Re-enactment and Medieval Fair was held to commemorate the 500th Anniversary of the landing of Henry Tudor. 'Henry' and a small group of his soldiers arrived by boat at Mill Bay. They were rowed ashore by local coastguards (in costume) and made their way up the rough terrain towards Brunt Farm. Despite the drizzly weather, they were watched by hundreds of spectators from the adjoining fields, many of whom followed 'Henry' (now mounted) and his entourage down the road to Dale. Many villagers, local organisations and visitors were in fifteenth century costume also and it was quite an impressive spectacle as the procession moved along the road. School children provided recorder music.

By the afternoon, the Medieval Fair was in full swing in Dale Meadow. The sun came out and there were demonstrations of jousting, sword-fighting, firing of cannon, etc also entertainment – dances, plays, etc – and a parade of entrants for the 'best medieval costume' competition. There were plenty of medieval side shows and refreshments and the 'pavilions' and banners made it a colourful and lively occasion.

Later, Lord Dynevor, a direct descendant of Rhys ap Thomas, unveiled the memorial stone on the south side of the village.

Some Dale villagers in their period costumes

Seafaring

SIXTEENTH and SEVENTEENTH CENTURIES

It is hard to imagine Dale without any boating activity and probably boats of some sort would have been used from the earliest times. By the time of Elizabeth I, Dale seemed to be quite a thriving sea-port. Sea-trading in Pembrokeshire had developed extensively. George Owen, writing in 1596 commented *"the country, especially of late years, is much fallen to trade at sea, and a great part of the country people are sea-men and mariners, and many of them continually abroad at sea, and seldom to be found at home"*! All sorts of foods, corn, wool, butter, cheese, even turnips were shipped to other parts along the coast and further abroad. Salt, wine, cloth and iron were imported.

Three vessels were reported as belonging to Dale:-
LE SONDAIE 8 tons, master Thomas Poell, with a crew of four men sailing to North Wales and Ireland to trade and *"a-fishing upp Severne"*. Another vessel, unnamed, whose master was Peter Holland, with a crew of four sailed as above. LE MARIE MOTTON, master Thomas Steven, with a crew of four sailing as above was the third. Another much larger ship, 40 tons LE GEORGE, was listed as belonging to St Brides but the part-owner and master was Thomas Poell, the same name as the master of LE SONDAIE. They could have been father and son or even the same person. LE GEORGE had a crew of twelve men and sailed southwards and to France.

The year 1566 has a very detailed report including the dates of sailings, names of ports visited and what cargo was carried. The information for Dale is:-
9th January 1566 : LE MARIE de DALE, master Thos Steven, carried from Milford Haven (ie the waterway) to Barnstaple 140m (ie measures) barley and 40m wheat for Richard Somer, St Brides.
1st February 1566 : LE MARIE de DALE, master Thos Steven, carried for Thos Laugharne, St Brides, from Barnstaple to Milford Haven 13cwt iron, 3 pieces calico, 60 yds dowlas (a coarse linen cloth) and canvas, 1 qr hops, 4 doz shoes.
20th February 1566 : LE SONDAIE 12 tons, master Peter Folande, carried from Milford Haven to Barnstaple 280m barley, 40m wheat for Geo Pryde, Haverfordwest.
23rd April 1566 : LE TRINITE, master Griffith David, sailed from Milford Haven to Barnstaple. She sailed again on 20th June 1566 and returned on 10th July with 3 tons pitch, 1t rosen (possibly used in caulking), 1 bolt canvas, 1 pk linen, 1 pk calico, 1 pk divers goods and also an unspecified quantity of brass.

Pirates and Smugglers

It was not long before 'privateers' began to make easy pickings by 'hi-jacking' cargo ships and selling the goods! Often the entrepreneurs who bought the stolen cargoes were Pembrokeshire gentry who turned a blind eye to their source.

In an attempt to stop the menace of piracy, a Commission was given the task of surveying the 'Ports and Creeks of Milford Haven' from 1550 onwards. Dale was reported as having 20 households – the Nangle, or Angle, had 30, Fishguard 20 and Tenby 200. The town of Milford Haven was not built then so Dale seems to have been the largest village, sometimes marked as 'ye towne of Dale' on maps and charts of the period, on the north bank of the estuary. The commissioners reported their discovery that there was a *"notable and knowen pirat within the haven of Milford". This ship had been there for three weeks and had "a crew of 40 men and a great deal of ordinance and hath of late taken 2 barkes, hath ryffled them and doth much harme and likely to do more…"*. Aboard the pirate ship were three men of Dale who were now under surety until further instructions were received.

Even worse happened in 1609 when the notorious pirate, Thomas Salkeld who had his lair on Lundy Island, sailed into the Haven and raided Dale, looting, robbing and setting houses on fire. The pirates made off with two fully-laden ships. Cannon shot has been found on Dale beach which may date back to this episode. The Pembrokeshire islands were a great haunt of pirates. In 1536 Skomer was uninhabited on account of the inclemency of the weather and pirates. These scoundrels also used to steal the islanders' cattle for their meat!

Dale villagers continued to earn their living from the sea throughout the seventeenth and eighteenth centuries. The profession 'Mariner' is regularly mentioned in wills and marriage registers; some of these may have been in the Navy. Several smuggling stories are told dating back to this period. Salt was very highly taxed and was often landed without being declared to Customs officials. The Brig is supposed to have been used to store contraband salt. In 1669 the DELIGHT OF SWANSEA was wrecked in Dale Roads below The Brig. Unfortunately, the cargo of salt she was carrying was ruined but the people of Dale managed to salvage the rest of the cargo… a large quantity of wine. More wine was retrieved from the wreck of LA MUETTE in 1757.

Dale had three Customs officials in 1810 and one, Rees Ingram, is named as a Revenue Man in early documents. Some officers used to patrol the coast while a Revenue cutter kept watch at sea.

LIGHTHOUSE

St Ann's Lighthouse is built on or near the site of an early, possibly medieval chapel. George Owen in 1596 records that St Ann's Chapel was *"three flight-shots west of the Haven's mouth and served as a landmark for ships approaching the Haven"*. The chapel was decayed – it may have been endowed by Henry Tudor on his landing at Mill Bay over a hundred years previously – but the round tower *"built like a windmill or pigeon house about 20 feet high"* remained. He does not mention a light but it is possible that in earlier times the priests of the chapel kept a fire or candles burning to warn shipping of danger or to show the way in to the Haven. The Brethren of the Blessed Trinity (forerunner of Trinity House) was one of the earliest religious orders to perform this service in Newcastle upon Tyne.

Trinity House, by now a country-wide chartered company with the rights to deal with navigation matters, was given permission to erect a light at St Ann's in 1662, though new buidings may not have been actually built. Pressure for an efficient light was growing in the early eighteenth century and Trinity House was granted a patent from the Crown on 15 March 1713. Dues of one penny per ton would be paid by British ships and two pence by strangers. The Corporation leased its patent rights to Joseph Allen of Dale Castle, the owner of the headland. He undertook to provide two lighthouses to work in conjunction as leading lights on a 99 year lease. Fires were used on top of the towers to give the light.

In 1800 two new towers were built with oil lamps replacing the coal fires. The new lamps were Argand Burners, using a current of air and enclosing the flame between concentric glass cylinders. The 'high' light is still standing in its position today, used until 1993 as a Coastguard Station, but the 'low' light was taken down and rebuilt in 1844 and is now the present lighthouse. Trinity House took over the running of the lighthouse completely on expiry of the lease in 1813.

The ruins of the old pigeon house tower must have been completely removed soon after the new towers were built but drawings/paintings were made before the demolition. Some excavation work was done when a new helicopter pad was being built in 1971 but no definite evidence has been found of the older buildings.

St Ann's was a profitable lighthouse with dues being collected in Liverpool, Swansea and Chepstow. After Joseph Allen's death, members of the family received part-shares in the lighthouse.

The round tower of St Ann's Chapel and Elizabethan Lighthouse

In the Census of 1841, three keepers and their families with 13 children between them lived at St Ann's. One of the boys, Thomas Owen Hall, later became a lighthouse keeper himself and married the niece of Grace Darling, the lifeboat heroine, when he was stationed in the North East of England. Thomas's grandson, Harold Owen Hall, also served as a keeper and was posted to St Ann's in 1950. His daughter remembers going to school in Dale including one occasion when she was blown off her bicycle whilst on her way to meet the Milford bus and all her books were blown about the headland. After that her mother requested a taxi for the St Ann's children which was fortunately agreed to by the Education Authority!

COASTAL TRADING

The MAYFLOWER used to sail from Williamston Park to Dale in 1795. Ale is supposed to have been exported from Dale. A building called The Brewhouse existed in 1705 probably on Dale Quay. In his Survey of Maritime History in 1748, Lewis Morris comments *"Ale is also noted for its fineness; they have several breweries and export considerable quantities of it… They also have plenty of herrings and mackrell upon this coast, which sometimes come up the Haven, as well as many other kinds of fish."*

Of Dale Road and Harbour he wrote *"This is a ready outlet for small vessels where they may ride in two or three fathoms at low water. The Pier, which lies now in ruins, would be very useful to trade if it was repaired."* A line of large stones stretching into the sea beyond The Brig and parallel to The Griffin wall is thought to be the remnants of the pier.

Coastal sailing vessels continued to work in and out of Dale throughout the nineteenth and early twentieth centuries on a commercial basis. They brought in heavy loads, not transportable by other means, usually grain, limestone, coal and culm – small particles of coal which was sometimes burned loose or often made into balls with cement. Culm was cheaper than coal and would be used to bank up the fire. The boats arrived on the high tide and when it went down would settle on the beach while the cargo was discharged.

The Rev Benjamin Davies, who kept all his receipts, took delivery of three carts of culm from Freystrop Colliery in 1804.

Mr Thomas Davies, Windmill Farm, ran a coal/culm importing business and his receipt books, dating from 1911, list the following boats which delivered to Pickleridge beach:-

MARY JANE LEWIS a 60 ton ketch built at Jacob's Yard, Pembroke Dock: She was actually owned by Mr Davies who traded with her until the 1930s, captained by Dick Gwilliam. In 1931 she sank in Swansea Bay after a severe buffeting in heavy gales and lost her rudder. The MARY JANE LEWIS was re-floated by Mr Davies's son, William, and Mr Sidney James before being sold to the Eynons of Angle who traded in sand and gravel. She was beached in East Angle Bay in the late 60s and her timber used to repair other boats. Only her ribs remained and in the 1970s these were burnt… a sad end for this well-remembered vessel.

ENID also made coal and culm deliveries.

GARLANDSTONE carried coal and culm from Hook and Saundersfoot Collieries in 1911-16: This vessel has been restored and can now be seen at Morwellham in Devon near to where she was built in 1903-9. Her first owner and master was Captain John Russan who lived at Musselwick. The Garlandstone was a large ketch, 76ft long and 20.2ft beam. She was oak-framed with pitch-pine planking, an elm keel and was the last but one wooden merchant sailing vessel to be built in Southern England. She had beautiful lines and was designed to carry a master and two crew with 100 tons of cargo. In 1912 she was fitted with an auxiliary paraffin engine but Captain Russan kept her rigged as a sailing vessel.

A coastal trader floating barrels of beer ashore for The Griffin : 1903

LIMEKILNS

Lime and culm was also delivered by boat direct to the kilns situated close to a beach. The limestone usually came from quarries in South Pembrokeshire. In Dale there were kilns at Castle Beach and Pickleridge where their remains can be seen today.

◀ Records show that in 1833 culm and stones were discharged for Mr George at Castle Beach and the same for Mr Lew Walters at Dale Kiln. In 1878 Mr Allen received 18 tons of limestone.

Lime was needed by the farmers as a fertilizer to dress the fields. It was prepared by being burnt in a furnace which would be filled up with broken lumps of limestone and culm. It was then set alight and after the very hot fire had cooled the residue was raked out and used as agricultural lime.

The kilns were owned by Dale Castle Estate and burners employed who lived close to the kilns. Sometimes one burner would travel round to two or three kilns. The limekiln at Castle Beach was last operated by Mr John Mathias who died in 1924, although the burning ceased before World War 1.

BOAT BUILDING

Boat building and repairing must have been carried on locally from very early times. There is a reference in 1387 to the rabbiting business on Skokolm and Skomer Islands where one of the costs involved was the repair of boat and also supplying new oars. Canvas is listed in the cargoes of boats from Dale trading in the sixteenth century and this may have been for sail-making. Shipbuilding increased in importance around Milford Haven after 1830 and two ships are listed as being built at Dale in the 1850s, totally 43 tons. There seems to have been a small boat-building business in Dale, then.

The 1851 Census shows there were 9 shipwrights and 6 shipwrights' apprentices living in Dale with several of these still working in 1881. William Reynolds, The Windmill, was a shipwright when in 1866 he married. His nephew, Seymour, also became a boat builder in Dale in the 1930s. Mr Seymour Reynolds is remembered for his well-crafted, clinker built, wooden fishing and sailing boats. His son and two grandsons continue the family tradition.

Until recently boats were built at the top of the beach using temporary cradles, etc then launched by slipping them into the water on a Spring tide. The Boathouse in Dale began life as a ships carpenters' workshop and boatyard. Boats were stored and repaired there until the late 1980s. *Back to sea after an overhaul* ▶

FISHING

Fishing is an occupation as old as Dale itself, if not older! Sea fish and shell fish have always been obtainable locally. In the sixteenth century small ships belonging to Dale went *"upp Severne a-fishing"*.

By 1810 fishermen in Milford Haven had to be registered, to comply with oyster fishing regulations. Seven fishing boats and their owners are listed from Dale:-

Name	Length	Owner
PASTORELLA	15 feet	John Rowe and Jemima Allen – married a naval officer in 1814
BETSY	13 feet	Thomas Hall – named as a mariner on his marriage certificate in 1793
TARTAR	18 feet	William Morris
MARY	15 feet	Jeremiah Hays, South Street – also a mariner when he was married in 1800
ROSE	16 feet	William Thomas, South Street
CHARLOTTE	16 feet	Philip Powell – Gent
ENDEAVOUR	16 feet	John Evans

Five men earned their living by fishing in 1841 including William Thomas, then aged 60, and Jeremiah Hays, then 70.

The next entries in the Oyster Fishing book are in 1865. Dale names were John Jones, a shipwright in his younger days, now landlord of The Griffin Inn as well as a serious fisherman, Tobias Codd and Thomas Sturley. Mr Sturley was born at Townsend in 1813 and was the father, grandfather and great grandfather of the much-talked of Sturley boatmen of Dale. Two of his sons were seamen, James born 1845, the father of four sons and four daughters lived at Townsend. Thomas, born 1846, had gained his master's ticket and was Captain of a deepsea trawler, the RACHEL. He had seven sons and five daughters. James's sons, Harry, Freddie and Isaac followed their father as lobster fishermen and were known as the Bottom Sturleys. Thomas's sons all went to sea; George, Peter and Bert worked on Milford trawlers while Edgar, John and Jim had a fishing boat at Dale. They were known as the Top Sturleys. There was friendly rivalry between the two families. Working from the 1920s-50s they put down pots around the coast between Grassholm and Linney Head. The lobsters and crabs were taken twice a week to Milford Fish Market and gurnard was brought back as bait.

Sometimes, if shoals came into the bay, herring, pollack, even sewin, were sold around the village. One of Thomas's granddaughters remembers the delicious fresh fish enjoyed at family suppers practically every day of the week. The nets were hung on the wall to dry and the brothers were often to be seen mending both them and the lobster pots. Needless to say they would often stop for a chat.

The Sturley's knowledge of the tides, currents, weather and boat handling was legendary. They often took visitors and supplies out to Skokholm. In the Top Boat, Edgar the skipper took the helm, Jim, who always wore a starfish badge in his trilby hat, was midships and John worked in the bow. A story is told of how they were once caught out by the weather and had to shelter in the lee of Skokholm for 48 hours with only a can of cold tea to sustain them.

Edgar and Bert ▶

Captain Thomas Sturley ▼

DISASTERS

The rocks and seas around the Dale Peninsula have from the earliest times taken their toll with loss of life and maritime craft; some of these have been covered elsewhere in this book, eg the DELIGHT and LA MUETTE in 'Pirates and Smugglers', two of the earliest recorded wrecks, and in others sections on 'Seafaring'.

Horrendous gales in November 1866 destroyed seven sailing ships entering the Haven. In pitch-darkness, fierce winds and driving rain the two vessels ALFRED ELIZA, French, and the COMMODORE, a barque taking coal to London, were tossed onto the rocks in Mill Bay, below St Ann's Head. *"Men manning the St Ann's lighthouse half a mile away, heard the anquished cries and hurried down the cliffs, risking their own lives to save the stricken crews."* Eight men escaped from one of the wrecks in an open boat, safely landing at Dale after battling though the elements. Many of the other men were rescued. Wreckage of the brigantine KING OF THE FOREST and the schooners ISABELLA and HOPE were found in Mill Bay and it became known as the 'Mill Bay Disaster'. It is supposed that the ELIZA AND MARY and the EGLANTINE *"sank in deepwater under the cliffs"*. Between 13.11.1866 and 1.12.1866 the Parish Burial Register lists the burials, presumably in the Churchyard, of 12 men found drowned, unknown, at Mill Bay. Between 1.10.1820 and 29.11.1918 the bodies of 49 men/seaman unknown were recovered and buried in Dale.

◄ Wrecks at Black Rock, one being the DEO GRATIA which found the MARIE CELESTE, December 1872 c1910

In April 1943 two landing craft with a major design fault and carrying 80 young marines and crew were refused permission to enter Milford. The LCG15 and LCG16 lost their battle against mountainous seas with the loss of 78 lives, helpless witnesses seeing the tragedy from above Blockhouse.

One of many potential disasters which ended happily was in 1972. The Captain of the German coaster LUX beached her on Dale beach in a storm. The crew were safe and well and she was refloated two nights later. ▶

Evidence of international disasters also come to our coastline. The Auxiliary Coastguard Log for August and September 1985 records wreckage and personal items, including parts of luggage rack, a leather suitcase, thought to be from the Air India 747 which crashed into the sea off the west coast of Ireland on 23 June 1985 with the loss of 329 lives.

On average two people annually lose their lives in swimming, diving, climbing accidents around Dale. Wrecks of past years still claim lives as divers explore these and run into difficulties. We are blessed with a great variety of beach, a dramatic coastline and wonderful opportunities to enjoy outdoor activities but the sea needs to be treated with respect using local knowledge and information to reduce the hazards.

COASTGUARDS

Originally HM Coastguard Service for Pembrokeshire was based at St. Ann's Head, Station HQ being located within the Lighthouse with a complement of six full-time officers under a District Controller plus auxiliaries. From 1966-93 one of two light towers was modified to serve as the Coastguard HQ with more modern equipment. In 1993 The Service moved to a new purpose-built Coastguard Maritime and Rescue Centre in Milford Haven with six full-time officers. This is manned around the clock with four Watches each with six staff in the Operations Rooms.

Dale Auxiliary Coastguard Station on Castle Way currently has a complement of 15 volunteers including Station Officer David Gainfort under Sector Manager, Dave Miller. The Dale Team covers a patch from Haverfordwest round to St Brides. Information on casualties is relayed to David from Milford HQ, the Police and other sources and appropriate action taken. When necessary the maroon is fired – a handheld rocket fired 1000 feet into the air to alert the Team. Call-outs average two each week. Regular patrols of the area are also carried out.

Training with the Sector Manager is regular and rigorous. Any auxiliary missing two consecutive training sessions receives a warning; a further session missed means dismissal from The Service. Training includes first aid, chart reading, also descending and ascending cliffs using a harness. This equipment can be operated by two auxiliaries only, one at the top and one being lowered; up to three can be brought up in the harness using the electric winch. Call-outs range from missing persons, drownings, trapped dogs, sailors, windsurfers and walkers in trouble to headline-catchers when ships run aground. Many of the village men have served in the Dale Team, receiving a number of medals and other awards.

Animal rescues can present special hazards. In recent years the same Magazine Store at West Blockhouse was involved when dogs slipped down the narrow channel into the Store below. On the second occasion Coastguard Auxiliary Warlow was volunteered and lowered down to locate the missing animal who promptly showed his appreciation by biting him on the hand through protective gloves! Someone else's turn to be an animal lover on the next shout, Steve??

As fierce gales swept Pembrokeshire on the night of Sunday 5 January 1936, the Lowestoft drifter the SHORE BREEZE with a crew of 10 was dashed against the rocks in The Vomit, St Ann's Head. The lights of a vessel had been spotted by Coastguard and Principal Lightkeeper W C Gilpin and the alarm raised at 7.25pm. Coastguard S O Patrick McIntyre reported *"Nobody could stand up there. I was crawling along the cliffs and I searched every nook and cranny, lying down and peering over"*. Nothing was detected until the Tuesday when wreckage on Marloes Sands was identified. Searches failed to reveal one survivor, William Harvey aged 32, who had scaled the treacherous cliffs to become wedged into the cliff face 60 ft up. He was spotted a week later by Angle Lifeboat and the body retrieved of this lone survivor trapped by an overhanging rock only to die of exposure before being reached. On the same evening the ketch, ETHEL MAY, was *"lifted like a piece of paper and crashed onto the rocks"* in Dale Bay. It is said auxiliaries from Dale were alerted by the Vicar in church; the 'best suit' of one of the auxiliaries was ruined in the search and rescue of John Kearney aged 67 and his son Robert. The father broke a leg when the rope to the breeches buoy snapped and he was dashed against the rocks.

August 5, 1973: The Liberian tanker DONA MARIKA grounded off Lindsway with 10,000 tons of high-octane fuel resulted in the evacuation of the the village of St Ishmaels. On arrival the problems facing the Dale Team were clear… no rockets could be fired, the strong Force 12 wind and driving rain making observation and rescue very difficult. The lifeboat made heroic but unsuccessful efforts to get in close. Then the Dale Team lowered ropes 195 ft down and despite expert advices they decided to go over the cliff to the now-exposed beach. The 38 Greek and Pakistan crew of the stricken ship climbed down a pilot ladder and were brought to safety by the Team, up the cliff path, frightened but very grateful.

Friday, February 17, 1996: Dale auxiliaries were involved in the recent disaster when the SEA EMPRESS with its cargo of 6,000 tons of crude oil came out of the channel approaching Milford Haven and onto rocks below West Blockhouse. *"Oil was spurting from the holed tanker, a rock the size of a minicar having breeched the vessel."* The Dale Team was called out but 'stood down', apart from the Station Officer, when their role became traffic and crowd control; S O David Gainfort spent several days supervising helicopter movements at St Ann's Head and in Milford, as well as large numbers of vehicles and people. At times the safety of those crowding the clifftop became more pressing than the disaster in the sea below!

Farms and Farming

WORK ON THE FARM

Living by and from the land has been an age old tradition in this area. The yearly round of sowing, reaping, milking and stock-rearing has gone on for centuries. Once the medieval, open field system was converted to individual, enclosed farms, methods of farming hardly changed until the nineteenth century and even then change was slow. Mixed farming was always practised.

Horses were still used for work until the 1950s; 40 were kept in 1930 and 18 in 1945. Oats, needed for feeding the horses, was the main crop in the early part of the twentieth century. Barley and wheat were also grown. Corn was harvested by horsedrawn Osborne binder and left in stooks until dry enough to be carried to the barn or rick for storage.

In about 1927 the first threshing machine made its appearance in Dale. Jimmy the Flags used to travel around with his steamdriven tractor engine 'The King of the Road', towing the huge thresher. There was great excitement when this fearsome apparatus made its appearance, though the work was hard and dirty. Threshing was always called thrashing in Pembrokeshire. During World War 2 a lot of permanent grass was ploughed in and cereals grown for the war effort.

One day Mr William Davies, a local farmer, arrived late for Home Guard duty in Dale Hut. Asked by his CO why he was late, he said *"I been a-thrashing"* to which the officer replied, *"Your wife, your girlfriend or who?" "Grain, for my country, Sir,"* was the answer!

Hay was also an important crop. During the nineteenth/early twentieth century, it was cut by horsedrawn mower, made and tossed using pitchforks and rakes. Neighbours, the women and even young children were called upon to help. When made, it was carted to the rick. Triples, an extended wooden frame, were put on the cart to enable a huge load of loose hay to be carried. Balers began to be used from the 1940s. From the 1950s sileage-making became increasingly common.

◀ *Longlands Farm (late 1920s): Mrs Emily Davies with daughters Dora and Elsie and water cart*

Brunt Farm (July 1947): Potato picking - having a break ▶

Early potatoes, which are such a feature of Dale farms today, were introduced in the 1930s. They were handset and handpicked. Later tractor-driven spinners were used to unearth the potatoes. As soon as it was time to lift, trailer-loads of women and children were collected from the village and taken to the field, all eager for the chance to earn some extra pocket money. From then on it was continuous, back-breaking work with a minute or two's respite, if you were quick, before the tractor came round again. Speed was essential; the earlier the potatoes were sold the better the price. All the workers were allowed to take a bag of potatoes home; tasty feeds of new potatoes in May/June are well-remembered.

Prompted by a government subsidy in 1932, sugar beet was grown but this ceased in Dale in 1942 as it was uneconomic. The factory was 160 miles away.

'Oldest Cow' aged 40 – Guinness Book of Records: Born Longlands Farm 1916, died 1956 and produced her 30th calf in 1955. Pictured with Miss Elsie Davies ▼

Beef cattle always out numbered dairy cows. There were two butchers in Dale in the 1840s and 50s. Milking was all done by hand and butter made from the surplus. In the cool farm dairy the cream was skimmed off, the whey being fed to the calves. The cream was churned in small glass churns. The larger farms used bigger wooden churns made by Llewellins Churn Works, Haverfordwest. The butter was taken by pony and trap round Milford and Hakin to be sold. At the beginning of August, villagers used to come up to the farms for free milk to make Dale Fair pudding.

Sheep, mainly Suffolks were kept for early lambs, though the ewes would be shorn in the summer. They were sometimes taken down to the Gann pool to be washed before shearing. Tack sheep were introduced on re-seeded potato ground in the 1960s.

Eggs were sold to local shops and poultry often went to the Haverfordwest Poultry Auction at Christmas. This was another busy time for local women who were needed as featherers. Farmers killed their own bacon pigs. Villagers sometimes had a pig's cot in their garden or court. The pig would largely be fed on household scraps. It was said that the moon had to be full or on the increase when the pig was killed or the bacon would not take salt and would spoil.

Rabbiting was another way of supplementing incomes, often using ferrets. Mr Tommy Reynolds from Marloes had a private taxi service taking the Dale lighthouse keepers' wives to Haverfordwest to do their weekly shop. He was also a buyer of rabbits from local farms. The women sat knee-high on rabbits going in but on their return there was plenty of room for themselves and the shopping, the rabbits having been despatched from Haverfordwest Station.

Many more farm workers were needed before mechanisation. In 1881, there were 19 agricultural labourers, 12 general labourers and 3 dairymaids living in Dale.

THE WINDMILL

The windmill tower on the north side of Dale was a working corn mill until about 1895. Mr Henry Sturley, Cliff Cottage, was the last person to remember the mill working. He died in 1975 aged 96. A windmill was marked at the site on Emmanuel Bowen's map of 1729. Many coastal landmarks are sketched in on this map, so possibly the windmill standing then was also useful in this way. The mill was rebuilt in the later eighteenth or early nineteenth century. James Reynolds, aged 55, was the miller living there in 1841 and his son, John, the miller until at least 1891.

The straight-sided, circular tower of the windmill is unusual in Pembrokeshire. It is a low, squat building with thick stone sides of a design traditional in West Wales. It may have had simple canvas sails attached to a cap which fitted over the roof. The cap was turned by a tail pole so that the sails faced into the wind. Captain Thomas Sturley, b 1846, whose father-in-law was John Reynolds the miller, used to go up to help turn the sails if the wind changed even though it might be 2 o'clock in the morning!

Mrs Ena Davies (nee Allen) and windmill tower

An interesting oral tradition exists in the village that a blind man was connected with the working of the mill. One version states that he was the supervisor of the building. He had been blinded during the Napoleonic Wars. It was thought he adapted the design from continental windmills. In another version it is the miller himself who was blind and supervised operations, using his keen sense of touch to set the millstones.

Several millstones remain from the mill's working days. Different types of stones were used for milling different grains. Two of the stones still at the windmill are hard, French burrstones used for milling wheat. It has also been recorded that millstones were shipped to Dale in 1698 and 1713.

CASTLE ESTATE and FARMHOUSES

During the seventeenth and eighteenth centuries Dale Castle Estate was built up by the Paynter and Allen families. The Paynter family, described as merchants, owned Broomhill in 1599. James Paynter, with his sons David and James, bought more land and property in Dale which passed by marriage and sale to William Allen, husband of Elizabeth Paynter, in 1699. On the death of John Allen in 1767 his land in Dale and elsewhere was inherited by his only daughter, Elinor, who married John Lloyd of Mabus, Cardiganshire in 1776. They both died in 1820 and the Estate has remained in the family since then.

According to the Tithe Map and Schedule of 1847, the Estate comprised 93% of the land in Dale. It was tenanted by farmers, householders and shopkeepers, etc.

Most of the farms and farmhouses on the Peninsula were established at least 250 years ago, and some may have been individual, compact holdings for several centuries. Snailton is a really old foundation and was mentioned as a holding (Snelleston) in a document of 1376; as with other properties, spellings vary eg Snailston, but is known locally as Snailton. Brunt Farm was allegedly named from Henry Tudor's words *"This is Brunt"* in 1485. The earliest dates for the farms are – Kete 1699, Moorland 1775, Point Farm 1749, Haggard Hay land 1734. Several parcels of land in early records include the word 'hay' in their names. It may have meant that it was a field surrounded by a hedge. Broomhill's earliest mention is 1558; it may have been renovated in the late eighteenth/early nineteenth centuries. It, and several other old houses in Dale, have massive chimneys typical of the region.

The Tithe Map and Schedule show that farmers to the north of Dale village held land in more scattered holdings. 12 farmers held between them over 100 small rectangular fields which were probably the remnants of the open township fields of medieval times. Some of these holdings had burgage rights such as the use of common land for pasturing animals. Gradually they were amalgamated, enclosed and brought into the ownership of the Castle Estate. A document of 1786 refers to *"land on Dale North Moor, called New Ground and 2 fields up on Moor Side, lately enclosed"*. This farm is shown as Moorside Farm on a map of 1814 but by 1847 had been merged with the newer Longlands Farm. West Point, Canthill, Hooks, Windmill and Spitland – Speedlands today – were all marked as 'new' farms by 1847. Longlands, West Point and Canthill farms are now buried under the former Dale Aerodrome.

The Estate employed its own carpenters and masons, also a gamekeeper. By an eighteenth century Act of Parliament, employers were required to obtain a gamekeeper's certificate. John Lloyd of Dale Castle bought his first certificate in 1784 at a cost of 2s 2d; by 1795 it had gone up to 3s 3d. Thomas Warlow was the gamekeeper in 1841.

Mount Pleasant with Gamekeeper William Johns, his wife and family in the foreground: Early 20th C

A gathering of tenants with Col Rhodri Lloyd-Philipps on the occasion of Hugh's 21st birthday : 1927
back row: Beatrice Davies, Maggie Bowles, Charlotte Gauld, Mary Sturley, Mary Roch, Evelyn Rind, Jack Davies, Jack Edwards, Harry Sturley, William Reynolds, Edgar Sturley
centre: John Edwards, John Young, Rosie Young, Hilda Young, Jack Edwards, Col Rhodri Lloyd-Philipps, Gladys Rind, Hannah Reynolds, Col George Rind, ?, George Roch, James Allen, Isaac Sturley
front row: Bessie Mathias, Polly Davies, James Sturley, Jane Phillips, Lewis Morgan, Tommy Davies

ALLENBROOK and DALE NURSERIES

◀ *Colonel George B A Rind and his wife on the occasion of their marriage:1909*

It is believed that several cottages occupied this site in the eighteenth century prior to the construction of Allenbrook in the early 1800s by the Castle Estate. This was one of two substantial, adjoining houses, the other being the vicarage. Sometimes Castle staff lived at Allenbrook or family members. On his return from service in India mainly with the 33rd Punjabi Regiment, Lieut-Colonel George Burnett Abercrombie Rind leased the properties and land from the Castle Estate. Following extensive conversion, he lived at Allenbrook from 1919 until his death in November 1958.

Those who know Allenbrook well, speak of it as being a warm and happy home with an 'atmosphere' of the past. It is reported that 'an elderly, bearded gentleman with grey hair' makes use of the library from time to time. A stocky figure in breeches and waistcoat, he has been seen relaxing in a chair but disappears as soon as eye contact has been made! No chill or threat is felt, rather a feeling of well-being. The library is in the old vicarage section of the house but 'the elderly gentleman' is thought to be a Rind family ghost not a man of the cloth. The BBC broadcast the Allenbrook ghost story in the 1950s.

Colonel and Mrs Rind were responsible for the layout of the excellent garden sporting a large variety of camelia bushes, belladonna lilies, wisteria – making a comeback – and a magnificent magnolia tree unique in Dale.

As well as taking a leading role in village activities, Colonel Rind and his family developed Dale Nurseries in the 1920s, building two large and two small greenhouses plus a cold house behind the now ruined Yellow Cottage on Castle Way, stretching west toward the Castle. This was *"a godsend to the village where there was little employment apart from farm labouring, fishing, and one or two jobs at the Castle. My cousin, Alan Goodridge (aged 14 years), left school on the Friday and started work at the Nurseries on the Monday"*, a story repeated by Cyril Thomas who left school in 1929 prior to his 14th birthday, Leslie Edwards and others. Jimmy Thomas from Jubilee, his four sons and two of his three daughters, all worked at some time for Colonel Rind, Jimmy leaving Dale Hill Farm to become Foreman for a number of years from the early 1930s.

Evelyn Jenkins (nee Gould) picking cornflowers (1938)

Kathleen Ramsbottom (nee Thomas), Marjorie Johnson (nee Sturley) and Edie Gilpin (nee Davies) with jug of homemade lemonade (1938)

The Nurseries provided fresh flowers, fruit and vegetables three times weekly to Carmarthen, Haverfordwest and Tenby markets before opening their own shops in Haverfordwest and Milford. This included wreaths. *"We often made 20 or 30 wreaths in a day. We grew no end of arum lilies."* Archie Thomas went by motorbike to get the orders which were delivered by lorry driven by Ivor Lloyd and Cyril Thomas. Archie was also ploughman. Marjorie Johnson (nee Sturley) remembers Jimmy Thomas grumbling, half-heartedly, when the girls' asked for 1/- bunch of chrysanthemums… *"That's not a shillings worth, more like a pounds worth!!"* Folk came on the 4 o'clock bus from Marloes, walking back, for tomatoes - *"half a pound only now"* instructed Jimmy – a cucumber and a lettuce. *"But it's a long way from Marloes for only half a pound of tomatoes and a cucumber!!"* *"It was hard work but we had some laughs"* Iris, Kathleen and Marjorie recall. They worked from 7.30am to 5.00pm. Marjorie's wages were 10/-s a week in 1938, rising over the years to 18/- after the War then a big rise to 25/- when wages legislation came in. Marjorie had £6 backpay and bought a posh new bike for £6-17-6.

The Company also had acreage under glass and in greenhouses at Crabhall Farm, Moor Farm and St Ishmaels and Colonel Rind was a forerunner in the Pembrokeshire early potato market. The girls remember packing them in half cwt wicker hampers ready to go by train from Haverfordwest to Birmingham.

When War broke out in 1939 the girls took over most of the jobs, including Land Army girls. *"They had their money, free board and were supplied with clothing – breeches, green pullovers, hats, lovely strong brogue shoes and stockings. We had to manage with what we could get at jumble sales. We'd none of the perks except a few extra clothing coupons. It used to annoy us."* During the War the sweet, juicy cucumbers were an alternative to sweets, even exchanged for a rare treat of a chocolate bar when the Church Army van called once a week.

Tremendous winds in the early 1950s caused extensive damage to trees, the greenhouses and property, then in September 1974 hurricane force winds and driving rain destroyed the greenhouses; Mr Bill Rind reported that he had lost almost £1,000 worth of tomatoes alone. This sadly saw the beginning of the end of the Nurseries in Dale but they and the Rind family are remembered with affection by many in the village. Villagers were invited to take away any flower pots and other items, any remaining glass having been used to repair the coldhouse to use as the last greenhouse.

Properties

DALE CASTLE

The earliest written record of the Castle was in 1699, when it was bought by William Allen. It seems probable, however, that there was a substantial stone building on the site well before that. This may have been a fortified manor house dating back to medieval times. No references have been found mentioning any battles or sieges at Dale, but a building here was garrisoned before Henry Tudor's arrival. In 1643, during the Civil War, Dale is mentioned as one of the places to be garrisoned by Lord Carbery, the Royalist leader.

The word 'Castle' in other Dale place names refers to the early coastal earthworks. Dale Castle has been the principal mansion house of the surrounding Estate for several centuries. The original building has been altered and extended during these years. The most recent renovation was in 1910 when the ground plan and exterior of the Castle was remodelled.

A large household and staff were needed to maintain the house and grounds. Census returns show that in 1841 when the owner's family was quite large, 13 staff including a governess lived at the Castle. Vegetables and fruit were supplied from the walled kitchen garden which has old fruit trees and a glasshouse with vine. Several gardeners were employed and also a coachman and grooms.

OLDER HOUSES IN DALE

There are several houses dating back to the eighteenth century in the village and a number of these are listed buildings. The houses near the Brig Quay were quite large and may have been occupied by more affluent mariners. Some properties near the Quay were used as warehouses. A terrace of smaller cottages lined South Street. Fishermen, labourers and paupers lived here in the nineteenth century. There were more cottages along the Dale Point Road sometimes referred to as Back Street, now fallen into ruins.

Ten cottages existed along the road leading north from Dale village known as Cliff Cottages, now demolished or rebuilt. North Street was listed in the 1841 Census with several more cottages. These were probably the houses clustered round Townsend. On a map of 1814 several buildings are marked in the fields to the west of Dale Castle and a Town Hall is mentioned in an earlier document in the west end of Dale Meadow.

Hill Cottage

Brook Cottage

Cliff Cottages

Military Presence

WEST BLOCKHOUSE

The West Blockhouse was part of the fortification of Milford Haven and Pembroke Dock initially to protect the kingdom from French and Spanish forces. In 1539 two circular blockhouses were begun but apparently not completed. Further development of these sites was not approved until 1850. Ordered by Lord Palmerston when Napoleon III threatened these shores and completed in 1857, this gun emplacement had six 10" guns, each weighing 95 cwt. Barracks for 41 men and one officer were solidly built of grey limestone and granite. In 1853 a newly qualified engineer officer Charles George Gordon posted to oversee the building reported - *"I have been doing plans for another fort to be built at the entrance to the Haven. I pity the officers and men who will have to live in these forts as they are in the most desolate places, seven miles from any town and fifteen from any conveyance."*

There is no evidence that in the nineteenth century West Blockhouse was ever garrisoned on a war footing. In 1881 three soldiers and their families were on site.

About 1900 it was decided to re-arm Milford Haven defences and a new Battery was built with two 9.2" B L Mark X guns and three 6" Mark VII guns; the original

battery was also given new equipment. This construction involved negotiations with the landlord and tenants of Brunt and other farms for the use of water…

In World War 1 West Blockhouse was designated a Counter Bombardment Battery and at last brought into active service with a troop of Royal Garrison Artillery stationed here.

The Battery was manned by the Pembrokeshire Heavy Regiment Royal Artillery (TA) during the Munich Crisis in 1938 and again in earnest a year later when War was declared. Its primary role was that of *"Examination Service for Milford Haven, but may be called upon to use its guns in the defence of the Port"*. The Battery also was the Control HQ for the Loop and Controlled Minefield, strung across the mouth of the haven. One officer's diary recorded regular mine-laying, minedropping operations by enemy aircraft with the destruction of shipping and loss of life. Other entries recorded regular ENSA Concerts, sports, parties and on January 20th 1941 *"Terrible day. Rain, rain, rain. Canteen roof off."*!

Between the Wars, the Battery was used for exercises. Brigadier Clifford Gough as a young artilleryman at West Blockhouse (1931-1935) maintained the guns with two other artillerymen and three civilians *"who came down from Pembroke Dock on the 'Duty Boat' on a Monday morning and returned home"* on a Friday afternoon. He recalls the interest caused by the delivery from Woolwich Arsenal via Pembroke Dockyard c1934 of a 9.2 inch gun barrel for

West Blockhouse. The gun barrel was loaded into the hulk of an old sailing ship specially purchased for the operation, towed to Dale where it was beached broadside at high tide. The side of the ship was cut away and eventually the barrel was mounted on a special trailer *"like a giant roller skate"* coupled to a large agricultural steam tractor. Problems occurred when the gun barrel jammed on the village shop corner! After a series of complicated manoeuvres, the gun barrel eventually made its way through the village only to become stuck on the Drift Hill, the tractor not being powerful enough to tow it up the hill! More complicated manoeuvres involving nothing more than ropes, baulks of timber, lifting frames and hydraulic jacks winched the trailer up in stages and on to West Blockhouse where the gun was mounted in the 9.2 inch battery.

After its closure and sale in 1959, The Landmark Trust purchased West Blockhouse and its extra-ordinary, even forbidding, setting in 1969. Following much clearance and restoration, visitors are now able to stay in the property fulfilling Brigadier Gough's wake-up call in the 1930s *"Come on, just have a look at the view; there are people who will pay pounds to have the opportunity"*.

DALE FORT

It was not until the latter half of the 1700s that Dale Point was fortified as part of the defences of Milford Haven, although this had been considered for 200 years. Batteries were placed behind earth banks *"which in 1780 had sixteen 24 pounders, two 6 pounders and lodging for fifty men"*. The current Fort, together with West Blockhouse, was planned in 1850 for Dale Point as part of the defences of Milford Haven against possible attack from Napoleon III. Lieutenant Colonel Victor, Royal Engineers, is thought to have designed these rather novel fortification, taking advantage of the natural shape of the rock they were built on and so deriving protection from it. Unlike West Blockhouse, this Fort had no gun emplacements but shell recesses for the seven 68lb guns and two 32lb guns for landward defences. *"There was also a drawbridge and in addition to the timber main gate still in place today there would have been an armoured gate with loops for musketry."* 20,000 gallons of water could be stored in two undergrounds tanks in front of the barrack blocks which could accommodate three officers and 59 non-commissioned officers, privates and 'women'.

Construction of the Fort was not welcomed by some in Dale including the squire of the Castle *"who owned the land and did not want the development to take place. The commander at Dale Point wrote to the squire to ask him to remove his cows as they were in danger of being blown up during rock blasting operations. They had been herded there deliberately to inconvenience and delay the building works."* In a letter to his brother, Charles Davies of Broomhill Farm wrote on 12 March 1855 *"The works at the Point are getting on very rapidly and you would scarcely know the old Point after being mangled in the way it is"*.

Dale Fort was not brought into active service until the end of the 1800s. However it saw 'action' during the 1890s when, in response to a realisation that the ordnance in situ could not penetrate armour plating effectively, a Zalinski's dynamite gun was brought from America for trials. Considerable alterations were needed to accommodate this new coastal defence weapon with a range of 4500 yards firing a 15 inch full calibre 1000lb shell. *"It was a brilliant solution to the problem of firing dynamite at enemy ships, it worked accurately and consistently but was soon overtaken by other developments."*

"By 1902 the War Office had decided to decommission the structure and it was sold in that year to Lieutenant Colonel A Owen-Evans RE which he converted into a private house" taking up residence in January 1911. The Fort was used in World War 1 but only as a signal station. The Colonel initiated alterations to adapt the Fort for family living.

"The family kept goats, bees and poultry and grew their own vegetables… fishing seems to have been a popular activity." Having filled eight boats with herring on one trip, the Colonel gave most of them to the villagers but decided to kipper a quantity. The Atlantic Fleet often assembled in Milford Haven, anchored off Dale Point. *"Follow me said Colonel Owen-Evans's eldest son Peter to his brother Anthony, I'll show you a trick. Peter was a trumpeter in the band of the Officer's Training Corps. He picked up his instrument clambered down to the shore and up on to the boom anchorage point. It was evening and getting dark; the lights of the Atlantic Fleet could be seen bobbing about on the water. The boy took a deep breath and blew 'lights out'. The lights of every ship in Dale Roads went out at the behest of a seven-year-old boy"*!

Mrs Owen-Evans, Pam, Peter and dogs Duke and Shot

Following the Colonel's death in 1925, the family sold Dale Fort to Miss M A Bland, Mab to her associates, who later married Colonel Lee-Roberts. Mab engaged in a number of diverse activities from breeding chincilla rabbits to canning mackerel caught locally in her 18 foot boat. Again concern for the defence of the Haven and the need to improve fire power led the Admiralty to comandeer the Fort, offering £100 per annum. Mrs Lee-Roberts wanted £110 per annum plus £13 per annum for chattels but there appears no record of the outcome. Operations began in 1942, the main work covering mine watching and de-gaussing, the latter aimed at reducing a ship's magnetic field to a safe level when in the area of magnetic mines. WRNS personnel operated the recording equipment and the results analysed by Dr James Huck and his assistant. Mine watching to ascertain precise bearings for the places where magnetic mines fell was carried out from the Mine Watcher's pill-box in front of the Operations Hut. *"At first this was done by two naval ratings, Wally and George. From 15 April 1943 they were replaced by WRNS personnel Rosalind Williams, Hope Elliston and Jessie Shepherd, who had trained together for the job."* The presence of young, attractive WRNSs enhanced Dale as a posting during World War 2 as well as the parties, mobile cinema and other social events.

Negotiations then began between Mrs Lee-Roberts and the West Wales Field Society who wanted a land base from which to service its Bird Observatory on Skokholm Island and to promulgate *"education and conservation of the unspoiled countryside of West Wales"*. A price of £6000 was agreed, with £300 of the Admiralty's compensation passed to the Society for repairs in February 1947. Wing Commander John Barrett was appointed to run the Centre and with Ruth, his wife, and their two children he moved to Black Rock cottage on 1 July 1947. Thus began the difficult task of repairing and preparing the Fort for its role but this was bliss when set alongside the hardships suffered as a prisoner-of-war in Germany. The first paying customers arrived on 20 March 1948 and school group on 22 March. Mr Barrett's first report (1948-49) stated that approximately 800 students had attended courses at Dale Fort and referred to *"the problems of teaching a class incapable of identifying a buttercup or too frightened to touch a tiny crab"*. The singular delivery of his lectures combined with his expertise and knowledge captured the attention of any audience.

One tragic event on 18 May 1960 affected all at the Centre as well as in the local community. A group sailing in the *Cubango* to Skokholm, passing the area used as a rifle range by HMS Harrier, heard a single shot followed by rapid fire. Before avoiding action could be taken the boatman, Harold Sturley, was hit in the throat and killed. Mr Barrett, his wife and four member of staff of the Field Study Centre immediately returned to Dale. At the Inquest it was said that *"NO red flag had been hoisted on the butts mast to warn shipping when firing started and NO proper look-outs had been posted to make sure there were no boats in the area"* also *"NO notices were put in the press warning the public of firing"*. The verdict of 'Accidental death' carried the rider that *"HMS Harrier failed to observe the conditions of Admiralty Orders in so far as it did not carry out standing orders"*.

In 1961 The Field Studies Council purchased Dale Fort from the West Wales Field Society. The demands on Mr Barrett's time from outside the Centre led to his decision in 1968 to take up new challenges. His successor, David Emerson, had been a student and a visiting lecturer at the Fort over a number of years. The profile of marine biology and maritime studies increased under his direction and a change of customer with less than half of the 2083 visitors in 1970-71 being sixth formers. Mr Emerson's retirement in 1995 saw the appointment in December 1995 of Julian Cremona, Head of Biology at St Mary's College, Southampton, as Director of the Centre. The Centre continues to thrive, providing educational opportunities for a wide cross-section of 'students'.

THE FLYING MACHINE

On a sunny May morning in 1912 the lighter 'Sarah' made her way in great secrecy from Avonmouth to Dale. John Evans writes *"The 'Sarah' was special, for she was carrying an unique cargo, one of 'them new fangled aeroplanes'; ...the strange craft was the Burney X2"*, a hydroped biplane constructed at Filton, Bristol from the ideas of Lieutenant C D Burney, RN. He had persuaded the directors of the Bristol & Colonial Aeroplane Group to refine and build the machine. As the Admiralty considered the work to be of strategic importance, a special 'X-dept' was setup.

Leaks and weight problems ensued. Minus the engine and towed by a torpedo boat, the X2 piloted by Lieutenant Bentley Darce, RN momentarily achieved success on 21 September before disaster struck. The X2 crashed on the water, the towline having been released too soon by the boat crew; Darce suffered little more than concussion. The damaged craft was returned to Bristol. August 1913 saw the new, improved X3 arrive in Dale for new trials but following some success the X3 ran onto a *"sandbank and was wrecked, bringing to an end a futuristic series of experiments"*.

Sir George White, whose great grandfather founded the Bristol & Colonial, and his namesake, visited Dale in 1998. He called on The Rev Malcolm and Mrs Beynon at the Vicarage whilst viewing the sites visited by his great grandfather in 1912 during the X2 trials. Sir George White, the elder, took an active interest in the project and was no doubt saddened when this failed. Needless to say his passion for flying machines of the future did not end with the X2 and X3.

WORLD WAR 1

Almost as soon as war broke out on 4 August 1914, troops began arriving in Dale for training. West Blockhouse was brought into full service for The Royal Artillery. The School (children on holiday), the Reading Room on South Street (soldiers' billets) and the new Vicarage (officers' quarters) on Castle Way were hurriedly comandeered, with many more troops camped in bell tents near the School and on the Meadow. Soon a large camp was built on Dale Meadow between Castle Way, the stream which runs through the Meadow, Dale Castle walled garden and Allenbrook Cottage. The hutted camp could barrack a battalion (1000 men) together with administrative, mess and training facilities, also a YMCA hut and hospital presumably with dental service… a pipe full of human teeth was unearthed in the thirities by gardeners at Dale Nursery! Some of the land behind and west of Dale Castle – Upper Dale Hill, The Hookses, Little Marloes and Longlands – was used to train for trench warfare. However, nothing could have prepared them adequately for the appalling sights and conditions of trench warfare in France and Belgium.

One of the first Battalions to camp at Dale was the 1/1st Brecknockshires of the South Wales Borderers, Territorial Force. They arrived on 28 September *"well over strength"* and with *"expectations of an early departure for France"*. The Battalion left Dale on 19 October and sailed from Southampton on 29 October 1914 not for France but India, where they remained until the end of the War. During their brief stay one soldier lost a cap badge, probably whilst training, which was unearthed during excavations of part of Great Castle Head, Dale in the Autumn of 1999 by the Dyfed Archaeological Trust.

brass Brecknockshire Battalion South Wales Borderers

The 2/1st Brecknockshire Battalion, South Wales Borderers, Territorial Force arrived in Dale in April 1915 until December 1915 when they moved to Bedford. As War progressed and the number of men increased to over one million, many were billeted in appalling conditions. Hutted camps like the one in Dale were used on a rotation basis to give troops some 'r and r' – rest and recuperation – from the hardships, with 'up-market' accommodation for a limited period. Dale was a very busy place; certainly it is recalled that the Church was full – *"a job for parishioners to find a seat"*.

Although no air raids were directed at Dale village, ships in the bay were in peril from enemy submarines and mines.

Training, Rest and Recuperation Camp on Dale Meadow during World War 1. Wounded soldiers from the Western Front were brought to the hospital here

The Armistice was signed on 11 November 1918. Plans for a Peace Celebration in the summer of 1919 were drawn up. Laddie Shepherd remembers speeches being made in the grounds of the Vicarage to a large number of the villagers, the Rev S B Williams being one of the main speakers. *"He had to leave again the same day as he was still in military uniform after serving overseas for a couple of years. Many villagers obtained jugs, cups, etc marked 'Peace 1919' that afternoon. People thought that peace had arrived for ever and there were great hopes of a better world. A firework display including rockets was held, together with a bonfire at the top of Dale Beach which was then a right-of-way for traffic, though not an official road."*

Fred Roch, one Dale son who returned was, like many, deeply affected by the 'War to end all wars' and rarely spoke of

his experiences, although had expressed the view he'd rather shoot his sons than let them go through the hell that was The Somme. A Royal Engineer, he was at Mametz Wood with the 38th (Welsh) Division in one of the bloodiest conflicts. He spoke of the crows ever-circling amidst the shelling and bombing. Amongst the carnage Private Roch was one day unexpectly hailed by another local lad, Walter Bevan, a stretcher bearer! In July 1987 a memorial column with impressive red dragon grasping the enemy's barbed wire was unveiled in memory of those who perished there in July 1916.

Forty men approximately went to War from Dale; five never returned having died serving their country overseas. After demobilisation was completed funds were raised for a village War Memorial in the Cemetery at the west end of the road going out of Dale. Sculpted by Mr Watcyn Jones of Llanybyther *"eighteen feet high and weighing nineteen and a half tons, the marble column supporting a white marble figure of a soldier standing at ease and facing the seas, is placed in the centre of Dale Cemetery"*. This was unveiled on June 19th 1923 by Major Gwilym Lloyd George MP for Pembrokeshire with hymns and prayers offered before a large congregation of local dignatories and Dale folk. The regimental band, a firing party and buglers of the 2nd Battalion The Welch Fusiliers took part in the ceremony with three volleys fired with drums rolls followed by the sounding of 'The Last Post' and the 'Reveille'. A number of beautiful floral tributes were placed at the base of the Memorial and on the graves of eight *"unknown heroes who were washed up by the sea at Dale, victims of the submarine warfare"*. A smaller monument had earlier been unveiled to their memory by Private H W 'Stokey' Lewis from Milford, holder of the Victoria Cross. Tea was served in the village hall, one of the last huts of the hospital unit on the Meadow during the War. A sacred concert in the open air followed in the evening.

Far from the land of their fathers these five sleep among the brave

1750 Private WALTER EDWARDS
1st Bn Welsh Guards
Fell at Passchendale: 1.12.1917 aged 26 years
Commemorated on Cambrai Memorial, France
Son of William and Susan Edwards, Townsend

76761 Gunner WALTER T EDWARDS – see page 55

78046 Private CLIVE V L REYNOLDS
15th Bn Durham Light Infantry
Died of wounds at Trier: 30.7.1918 aged 19 years
Cologne Southern Cemetery, Germany Plot 14, Row E
Son of John and Hannah Reynolds, Richmond House

64876 Bombardier ARTHUR EDWARDS, MM
12th Bty 24th Bde Royal Field Artillery
Fell at Ypres: 25.3.1918 aged 27 years
Commemorated on Arras Memorial, France
Son of John and Catherine Edwards, Moorlands

46477 Private JOHN CODD
9th Bn Welch Regiment
Fell at Messines Ridge: 7.6.1917 aged 27 years
Commemorated on Menin Gate Memorial, Ypres
Son of Thomas and Sarah Codd, Eaton Hall Lodge

76761 Gunner WALTER T EDWARDS
298th Siege Bty Royal Garrison Artillery
Fell at Poperinge 23.12.1917 aged 29 years
Buried in Nine Elms British Cemetery, Belgium Plot 13, Row B, Grave 5

Son of Richard and Elizabeth Edwards South Street, Dale

STREET COLLECTION
ON BEHALF OF
F.M. EARL HAIG'S APPEAL
(APPEALS DEPT. FOR BRITISH LEGION).
26, ECCLESTON SQUARE, LONDON, S.W.1

No 24244

DATE Nov. 10 1926

THE BEARERS Misses Allen & A Thomas
are A FIT AND PROPER PERSONS TO ACT AS A COLLECTOR ON THE ABOVE NAMED OCCASION, AND are HEREBY AUTHORISED SO TO ACT SUBJECT TO THE CONDITIONS ATTACHED TO THE PERMIT ISSUED BY THE POLICE AUTHORITIES (OR WATCH COMMITTEE) COVERING THE DISTRICT OF

(DISTRICT) Dale

ON BEHALF OF
Capt. W. G. WILLCOX, ..., Organising Secretary.
F.M. EARL HAIG'S APPEAL

ISSUED BY

N.B. THIS CERTIFICATE MUST BE PRODUCED FOR INSPECTION BY ANY POLICE OFFICER ON DEMAND AND RETURNED TO THE ORGANIZERS WITH THE COLLECTING BOX

No. 10

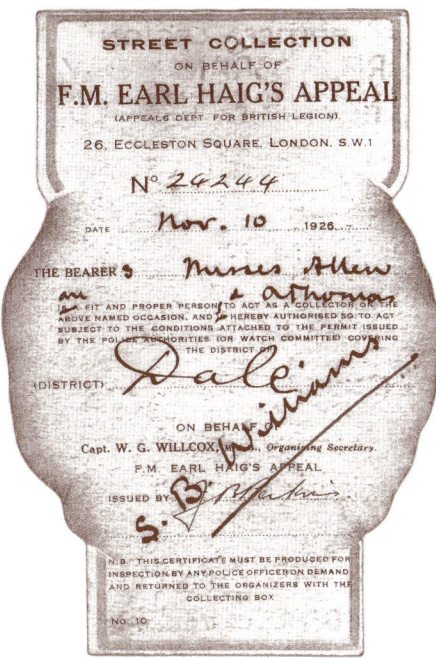

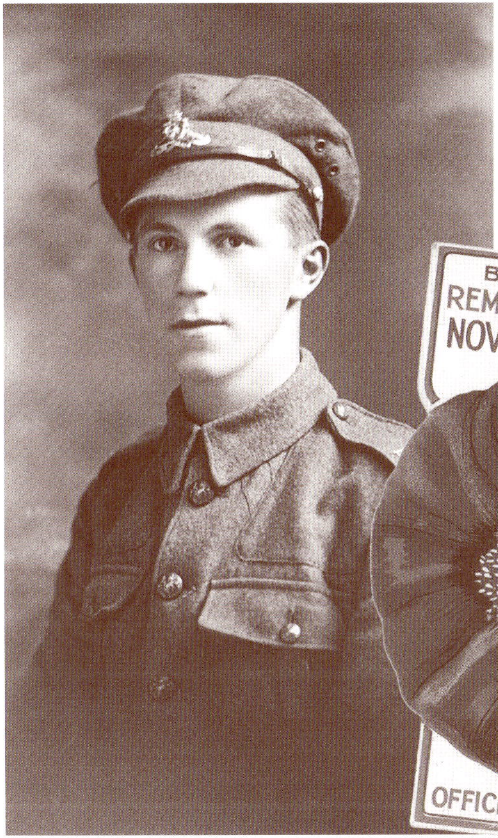

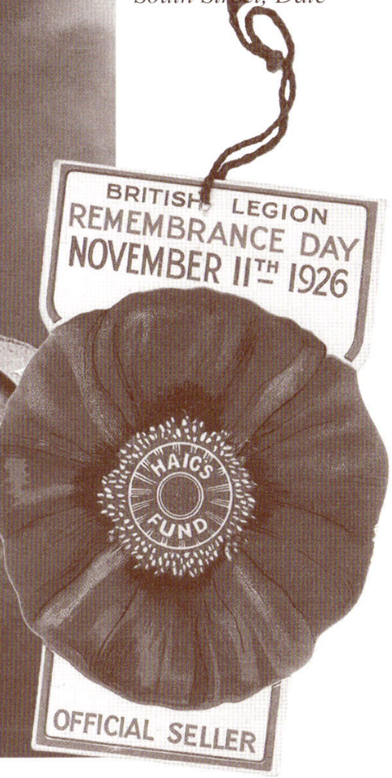

WORLD WAR 2 and beyond

The outbreak of war on 3rd September 1939 when the British Expeditionary Force began leaving for France, saw Dale once again become 'militarised' as local men joined up or were conscripted. Areas in and around the village were prepared to receive troops to provide protection from invasion and for the Haven.

Dale Fort and West Blockhouse were once more brought into service, the latter already occupied by the Pembrokeshire Heavy Regiment Royal Artillery (TA) charged with using its guns in the defence of the Haven, together with the Royal Artillery Battery established at St Ann's Head both under the Fire Commander. The Admiralty comandeered the Fort from the owner Mrs Lee-Roberts. The sites were mainly involved with the detection of mines and the protection of shipping from mines. A Decoy Battery was established near Watwick Point between Blockhouse and the Fort. Also a number of Anti-Aircraft Gun Batteries (ag) and Searchlight Batteries (s) were established to the north of the village and around the perimeter of the Peninsula.

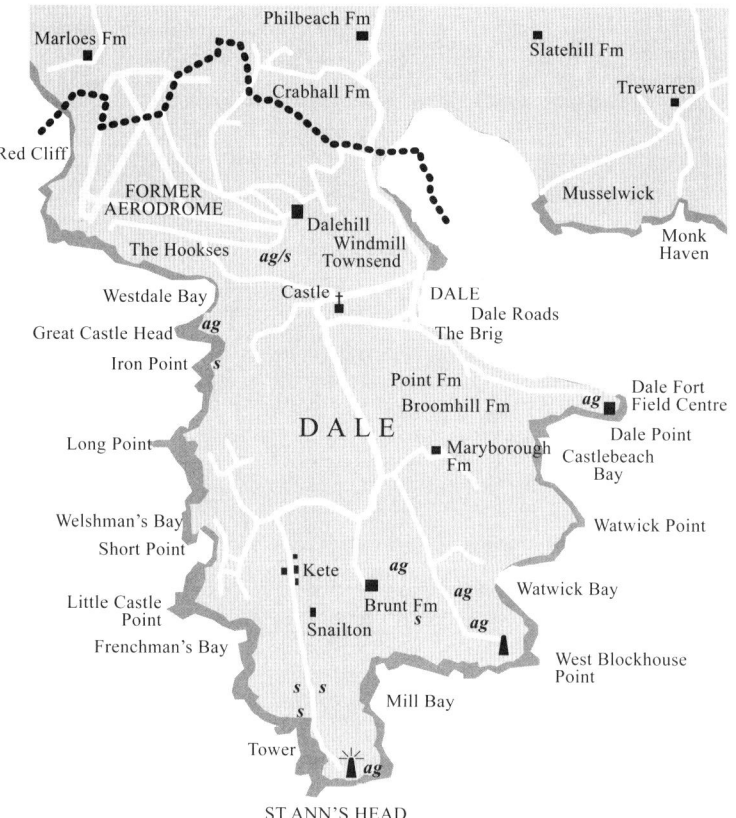

As war began the Royal Air Force (RAF) moved to a site north of Dale, then at Snailton, and the Royal Fleet Air Arm (RFAA) at Kete together with the Royal Observer Corps (ROC), the RAF providing a base for coastal defence aircraft and the RFAA and ROC a radar station and meteorological centre. An air raid shelter was constructed at Dale School.

West Blockhouse and St Ann's Head were garrisoned with Royal Artillery officers and men. Both positions afforded excellent views of sea and sky, invaluable for the early detection of the enemy. The two lighthouse buildings at St Ann's Head, 'high' and 'low', were the HQ of 532 Coast Regiment and of the Fire Commander (FC) responsible for early warning and control of the fire of the batteries. These defences were commanded in 1939 by Colonel Foster. A number of trawlers and minesweepers and two examination vessels patrolled the waters. Unknown vessels wishing to enter the Haven were challenged from St Ann's Head to identify themselves in Morse Code. Any vessel failing to give the appropriate signal would, at the discretion of the FC, receive a warning shot across the bows from Blockhouse.

The Haven was a convoy assembly point and hosted an RAF flying base for Sunderlands and Catalinas. These attracted attention and mines were frequently laid by enemy aircraft, the raids being at night and mostly on moonlit nights. The mines could be spotted drifting down supported by blue nylon parachutes – highly dangerous; many missed the water and exploded on the rocks below. German aerial minelaying increased dramatically toward the end of 1940, its first casualty being the DAKOTIAN sunk in Dale Roads on the 21st November, followed by the sinking of four more vessels before the end of the year. The War Diary of West Blockhouse for January 1941 confirms the intensity of the mine-laying and bombing. In the early days the only guns that enemy bombers had to face were the machine guns.

April 1st 1941: SS ADELLEN bombed and on fire. I actually saw a German plane bombing the ship. A number missed but at least one hit and started a fire. I was impotent with rage. It was broad daylight and we had nothing to throw at it.

(Extract from 2nd Lieutenant White's diary)

Also in April 1941, 20th and 22nd, Brunt Farm sustained much damage from bombs which had landed nearby… well remembered dates as Mrs Davies gave birth there to her second daughter, Pam, on 21st April. Nearby was **Brunt Camp**, in the calves park, field 405, with tents for the soldiers. One October night in 1941 fierce winds and rain flattened the tents, the soldiers taking refuge in and around the farmhouse and outbuildings with Mr and Mrs James Allen and Mr William Davies. Shortage of repair materials meant rain coming into the farmhouse. The soldiers trying to dry out and the family moved buckets around to catch the rainwater whilst trying to avoid getting wet… pick a spot then all change!!

Dale Airfield was constructed in 1941 and opened in June 1942 as a satellite of RAF Talbenny. The Station's first Unit the 304 (Polish) Squadron arrived from Tiree, Scotland on 15 June with their Wellington Mk1c bombers. The duties of the Squadron were anti-submarine and shipping patrols over the South Western Approaches and the Bay of Biscay. During these patrols Squadron aircraft were frequently attacked by German aircraft with several air battles; on 9th February 1943 Wellington W5718 with Sqn Ldr E Ladro and his crew successfully beat off an attack by four JU-88s which lasted 58 minutes. Despite many hazardous operations all 304 Squadron's losses were due to bad weather or mechanical failure. The Squadron transferred to Norfolk in March 1943. On 3rd January 1943 the roar of thirty bomber aircraft of the US 8th Air Force filled the skies, an awesome sight and sound! Following a raid on U-boat pens they were looking for somewhere to land. Four B-17's landed safely at RAF Dale; sadly within three months all but one had been lost in action. The Coastal Command Development Unit took over the airfield in April 1943.

The Western Telegraph

At 3.20 am on August 12th, 1942, Vickers Wellington HX384 of 304 (Polish) Squadron took off from the RAF Station at Dale on a routine operational sortie. Watching from a second aircraft, Flight Lieutenant Edward Zarudski saw the navigation lights dip below the cliff at the end of the runway. The twin-engined Wellington reared up and veered sharply to the right before dropping below the cliffs. Just 30 seconds later there was a flash followed by a glow and then darkness. The crash claimed the lives of the six crew members and their bodies were later recovered from the wreck.

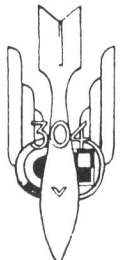

In August 1984 Professor E Zarudzki organised a wreath-laying on the sea to commemorate the six Polish airmen who had lost their lives off the cliffs of Dale.

7th September 1943 saw Dale Airfield taken over by the Royal Navy and renamed HMS Goldcrest, its role being concerned with training. Until its closure in December 1947, no less than nine Squadrons – 748, 762, 784, 790, 794, 809, 861, 897 and 1770 – served here flying Defiants, Fulmars, Masters and Martinets, Blenheims, Beaufighters, Wellingtons and Mosquitoes, Fireflies and Ansons.

Snailton, manned during part of the War with RAF and Army personnel, including some Jamaican lads, was rather a mystery. It is said that secret operations and tests took place there?

Kete was established early in the war as RAF Kete and as a radar station for the detection of low flying aircraft and surveillance of the sea surface. Kete is, however, best remembered for its a) Royal Naval Aircraft Direction Centre whose purpose was to train air direction officers and radar plotters for service on aircraft carriers, etc and b) School of Meteorology training instruction officers and observers. It was commissioned in 1944 as HMS Harrier. As aircraft could not be spared from the war at sea for training use, the Navy requisitioned ice-cream tricycles instead.

"Each trike was fitted with a radio telephone, compass and a musician's metronome to beat strict time. Ridden by rating or wrens, one trike could be the 'enemy bomber' and others were 'Fleet Air Arm fighters'. The bomber pilot would steer a course by compass, pedalling in time with the metronome to maintain the given airspeed. Watching from the distant 'carrier' the trainee Air Direction Officer would calculate the bomber's course and speed and radio orders to the 'fighters' to guide them in to intercept and 'shoot it down' before it reached its target."

Kete is an isolated location exposed to the elements, details of which are graphically remembered by many who served here. During the harsh winter of 1947 the Station was cut off from the rest of the County, bread and milk being brought into Dale by sea. In November 1954, a hurricane caused damages estimated at £7,000 to HMS Harrier. The Met Office at Kete recorded a wind speed of 106mph. Kete is also remembered as a wonderful setting in good weather for sports, sunbathing, etc. *"Then, of course, there was the Wrens' special contribution to Harrier's attractions; I remember the Fire Party regularly having to be piped to muster from the heather and their girlfriends on warm summer evenings!"*

Wrens formed the majority of personnel with as many as 240 ship's company and trainees on board at one time. The wrens had their own fenced-off accommodation consisting of long, low, brick buildings with corrugated iron roofs connected by corridors. Each room accommodated 12 wrens with a separate room for the Leading Wren-in-Charge. Loose wires and well-worn paths between the wrens and the ratings accommodation told their own story!

The local community joined many of the social occasions at HMS Harrier with dances, concerts, drama by the Kete Repertory Company, etc in the Officers' and Ratings' Messes. The Annual Children's Christmas Party saw children from Dale and the surrounding area eagerly converge on Kete; in 1954-5 'Dan Dare – Pilot of the Future' visited the Party accompanied by fireworks and other thrills. There was an Annual Sports Day, succeeded by an Annual Navy Day, with sports, a fair, a band, a dance and air display among some of the events on different occasions. One incident which deterred village girls, briefly, from attending functions on dark evenings was the White Lady of Drift Hill – the road just beyond the Cemetery going to St Ann's Head. The story tells of a white, misty shape emerging from the woods into the centre of the road and a scream heard before the apparition slowly floats back into the woods! Some versions tell only of the emergence from the wood …. before they 'legged it' back down Blue Anchor Way!!

HMS Harrier, as with other Naval stations, was run as if it were a ship – when leaving 'ship' you 'caught the liberty boat ashore' at certain times. There was a Church on camp and all 'on board' were expected to attend Sunday morning service. One forces tradition consistent throughout the services is that of the officers serving Christmas lunch to the other ranks. Here we see Wren officers serving the wrens in the Galley on HMS Harrier.

December 1960 saw HMS Harrier close.

Royal Naval Sick Quarters, the main site being on HMS Goldcrest at Dale Airfield, consisted of a long, brick building with a two-bedded ward leading off; male patients were nursed in a separate two-bedded ward. Every morning the Medical Officer held Outpatients in a small ward equipped for minor surgery. Anything more serious was transferred to Haverfordwest County Hospital. However, in an emergency, patients could be treated as the Staff were well-qualified to deal with such events –
Staff, Dale: 1 Surgeon Lt Commander RNVR; 1 Surgeon Lieutenant RNVR; 1 Senior Nursing Sister QARNNS; 2 VADs RNVR
Staff, Kete: 1 Surgeon Lieutenant RNVR; 2 VADs RNVR.

HMS Harrier was called upon to provide representatives at many formal engagements, one being the annual Remembrance Day Service and Parade in Milford Haven and at the War Memorial in the village. One Dale son, James Lloyd, lost his life when a mine-sweeper was bombed by a German aeroplane in the North Sea in 1940. He had lived with his grandfather, Mr John James, at Cliff Cottage and worked on farms, his last The Windmill. His name has been added to the War Memorial to be remembered always.

LT/JX 170660 Seaman JAMES ARTHUR LLOYD
HM Trawler Fifeshire, Royal Naval Patrol Service
Lost at sea 20.2.1940 aged 22 years
Commemorated on Lowestoft Naval Memorial,
Suffolk: Panel 2, Column 2
Son of Sidney and Winifred Lloyd of Dale

HMS Harrier c1950: Wonderful Wedding said to have taken place at Dale Congregational Chapel

Faith and Education

ST JAMES' CHURCH

The Parish Church, dedicated to St James, is thought to be of medieval foundation with the chancel and nave dating back to the thirteenth/fourteenth century. The tower has original barrel vaulting, window lights, stair doorway and parapet dating back to around 1500. This might have been a landmark tower with the east and west facing top storey windows lit at night as an aid to navigation.

The first recorded mention of the Church was in 1291 when a valuation known as the Taxatio was made of most churches in order to finance Edward I's intended Crusade. Dale Church was valued at £5.6.8. At the same time, Marloes was valued at £16.0.0, St Brides £13.6.8 and St Ishmaels £8.0.0. Other early records are very meagre but include the following:-

1513: A royal writ of Henry VIII appointed collectors for the *"Defence and Protection of the Anglican Church ...to allay and extirpate heresies and schisms in the church universal which in these days flourish more than usually"*. Dale was one of the churches which was excused payment on the grounds that they were *"diminished, impoverished and destroyed by wars, fires, ruins, inundations of rivers and other misfortunes and chances"*. In 1517 Dale with Marloes and St Ishmaels was again excepted from payment.

1543: Another levy was made by the crown, this time *"to be gathered by the devotion of the people for defence against the Turk"* and Dale was not excepted. There were 14 contributors in Dale.

1587: A silver chalice was given to the church.

The church was in the hands of the Crown by 1594 having formerly belonged to the Priory of St Thomas, Haverfordwest. Reference was made to the chancel being in decay as no farmer had been charged to do the repairs. The tithes, some of which were paid in fish, were not very productive as the inhabitants *"were not so well able to occupy that trade"* as formerly.

The Rev SB Williams, 1910-1928

St James' Church, Dale c1885

In 1688, the Dale incumbent did not offer a catechising service as he could spare no time!

The church was rebuilt in 1761 at the sole expense of John Allen, Esq, of Dale Castle, who also presented a font and altar table of Italian marble.

One of the earlier parsons who left some documentation was the Rev Benjamin Davies c1795-1819. He seemed to be quite an active gentleman and had a boat to get to St Ishmaels; he bought horseshoes in 1803 and in 1805 stangs of hay, a saddle and Pelham bridle, not to mention shot, powder and four gallons of beer! Other receipted bills show that he belonged to Haverfordwest Circulating Library in 1791, bought several amounts of material, buttons, ribbon, lace, tape and a tailor made for him four coats, several breeches and waistcoats. He bought Souchang tea from Haverfordwest .... perhaps it was not stocked by the village shops!

By 1833 the Church was in the patronage of J P A Lloyd-Philipps, Esq. More work was done on the building in the late nineteenth century including re-roofing and re-flooring. At this time the church had a gallery at the west end, was plastered internally and also had Royal Arms on the walls in addition to the memorial tablets which are still there today. Further work was done in 1890, including excavating away the building-up from the graveyard and putting in drainage. The gallery and its seats were removed, the floor was re-tiled and the ceiling, pews and pulpit put in. An American organ was installed and the bell re-hung. The bell was made by Llewellins & James of Bristol in 1874. The plan to build a new porch over the door never materialised after the original porch had been pulled down in 1890.

It had been common for vicars to serve other parishes in conjunction with Dale before 1898 but from then until 1975 the vicar had charge of Dale only. The Rev. S. B. Williams, 1910-28, was often known as the sporting vicar. He had played rugby for Llanelli for several seasons in his younger days and had a passion for cricket. He served as a military chaplin in World War One and was one of the first in Dale to own a motor car. After 1920, when lay patronage of the living ceased and the Church in Wales was disestablished, the onus of fundraising was placed on church members and this took the form of concerts, fetes, whist drives, etc as it does today.

CHAPELS

The Congregational and Wesleyan congregations were part of village life in the past. The Congregational Chapel stands on The Brig Quay, having been converted into a private home, whilst the Wesleyan Chapel is said to have stood on or near the site of the School House on Castle Way another private home.

John Wesley visited Pembrokeshire regularly in the 1760s, '70s, '80s and '90s. It is recorded that he visited Dale on 21 August 1771 ▶

Did his harsh words stir the preachers to greater action and the people to be concerned?

A Wesleyan Society was formed at Dale in the 1790s and *"a chapel built in 1809 with a ground rent of sixpence a year"*. One of the regular preachers was shopkeeper, Mr Spriggs, of Rose Cottage.

> **"A Peep Into The Past"**
> **TODAY IN 1771.**
> **JOHN WESLEY'S VISIT TO DALE.**
>
> "August 22nd, 1771: I rode to Dale, a little village at the mouth of Milford Haven. It seemed to me that our preachers had bestowed here much pains to little purpose. The people, one and all, seemed as dead as stones—perfectly quiet and perfectly unconcerned.
> I told them just what I thought. I went as a sword to their hearts. They felt the truth, and wept bitterly."

The preacher most associated with Dale Wesleyans was Mr Thomas Henton Calverley (b. 1816, d. 22.11.1889 at Dale Fort). The 1881 Census gave his occupation as "Wesleyan Home Missionary", birthplace Melton Mowbray, Leicester and dwelling at the Brig Inn, Dale. Mr Calverley so frequently used the steep path behind the Brig Inn into Blue Anchor Wood to visit Merryborough and Broomhill farms that it became known as Calverley's path and later Calvary path. The Calvary name suggested to some a connection with the Crucifixion and Calvary Hill due to the steepness of the hill and a cross on top! From the early months of 1889, he conducted services on alternate Sunday afternoons and evenings at Dale and Marloes, though his efforts were to end when he died in October that year "In great peace" aged 74 years. No doubt the stress and strain of travelling pre-motor car, together with that of preaching had its effect on Mr Calverley. Although other local preachers filled the breach it is said "at Dale the Cause was failing". The Dale chapel did not appear on the Circuit Plan in January 1904.

The Congregational Chapel was built in 1838, its founder being James Palmer, a Milford Haven draper. His father had been a light-keeper at St Ann's Head lighthouse. Mr Palmer is buried in Dale churchyard. The building appears on the 1847 Tithe Map (154) as House and Meeting House.

In the earlier years Dale was one pastorate with Little Haven and later St Ishmaels. Theophilus James (1846-1879) and Rhys Price (1911-1936) served the community for 33 years and 25 years respectively. Mr Price was a miner before training for the ministry and first ordained in 1904. He married Miss Ethel Richards of Winterton, Marloes. Mr Price retired early through ill-health and his successor Archibald J Harries (1938-1943) are the two Congregational ministers remembered today by senior villagers.

The Dale Congregational Sunday School Register still in existence for the years 1915-1928 – 1918-1919 not recorded – shows fluctuations in numbers registered and attending. 21 girls and 11 boys were registered in January 1915, the number of boys reducing during 1916 to only 2 and 8 girls in September 1917. Some of the boys were called up for active service and tragically young Clive Reynolds, who had played the organ in Chapel, lost his life. Clive is commemorated on the Dale War Memorial also a commemorative plate which had been in the Chapel is part of the family grave in Dale Cemetery. Following World War 1, attendances increased including a number from the earlier years. Sunday School was then not exclusively for the youngsters. Sunshine Corner organised by Mr and Mrs Stanley Duffield replaced the traditional Sunday School in the late 1960s; this proved popular with the local children.

During World War 2 a group of servicemen retired to Brook Cottage after Chapel to continue their songs of praise. David Norgate, Royal Navy, preached here, met a local girl, Marion Reynolds, whom he subsequently married.

After World War 2 and a succession of ministers, attendances dwindled until final closure in the early 1960s. China with the Dale Congregational Chapel motif was gifted to the Dale Women's Institute and is still regularly used at meetings. The Chapel was converted in 1976 to a private dwelling and to date is occupied by the purchaser.

THE SCHOOL

Day school education in Dale may have begun around the middle of the last century. Ann Stephens, aged 60, was listed on the 1841 Census as a schoolmistress living in North Street; she may have run a dame school, teaching very elementary reading and writing. By 1846, there was a Mrs Bevans School in Dale. It was established under a charitable trust to provide some education for children living a long way from existing schools. 72 children were on the roll when an inspection was carried out soon after the school's foundation. The school building was a former corn store lent and furnished by the landowner Mr Lloyd-Philipps.

Education was made compulsory in 1870 and Dale School was set up in accordance with the new law. A completely new building, still used today, was finished in 1876 when Mr William Edwards was appointed Headmaster. He was assisted by a sewing mistress on two afternoons per week and by monitors and monitresses. These were ex-pupils who acted as untrained teachers at a very low salary. They would often go to training college after a few years. In 1889, Catherine Roch was described as a monitress but by 1898 she is Miss Roch, the Infant teacher. All children were taught in the main schoolroom; in 1895 an extension was added as the Infants' classroom.

School holidays were quite different from nowadays. There was a three week holiday beginning towards the end of August and about a week around Christmas, though some years the school was closed on Christmas Day only. However day and half-day holidays were very common the reasons being funerals, fair days, bazaars, cricket match, tea parties, WI outings, Guide outings, the circus. During World War 2 holidays were given for fruit and potato picking. Afterwards these extra holidays became less common.

From 1946 all the children over the age of 11 were taken by bus to secondary schools in Milford Haven. Before that time, a few children had gone on scholarships or as fee-paying pupils to the Grammar and Central Schools in nearby towns. They used to live 'in digs' during the week.

Early Class Group Photographs: c1900

Extracts from the Headmaster's Log make interesting reading:-

16.2.1883	Mr I Thomas visited the school to make a complaint of some of the boys throwing stones on his pig's sty. I promised to undertake to put a stop to the practice and this promise pacified the old gentleman …though when he came, he was wild with rage.
24.5.1892	School closed because of an epidemic of measles.
14.3.1903	Some brushwork apparatus arrived this morning. A beginning of the subject will be made next week. The scholars seem delighted with the thought of brushes and paint.
5.3.1916	Very cold for scholars – grate too small for large room. Temperature keeping around 40 degrees.
2.3.1918	First days work on garden. Wednesdays and Fridays to be gardening days 2.30-3.30pm.
15.1.1920	Master (Mr J Dale) absent. Bicycle broke on way to school.
5.12.1927	Very dark morning – no written work possible.
2.6.1931	Mrs Pickerell addressed the children on temperance.
25.5.1933	The older children are to have swimming instruction today (from Brig slip!)
23.4.1937	Beautiful day so school journey to Castle Beach leaving school at 3pm.
3.9.1939	School re-opened today having been closed during last week for National Emergency. Children all carry gas masks and have daily practice in their use.
17.4.1942	Application made for equipment necessary to the proper cooking and serving of the mid-day meal.
6.3.1950	No transport from St Ann's – no petrol.
6.9.1955	School re-opened with 58 on books. Highest number for many years (RNAS Kete open).
16.11.1957	New building ready for occupation (with indoor flush toilets for the first time).
12.7.1958	Official Opening Day. Pageant by children. Speeches by guests.
23.4.1963	19 children admitted from Marloes V.C. School which closed permanently at the end of last term.
12.2.1970	Overnight snow – no school bus – no electricity – no milk – no pupils.

Dale Primary School: Coronation Pageant 1953 ▶

Terrance James
Dennis Gainfort
?
Angela Thomas
Mary Richards
Raymond Richards
Michael Pawlett
Alan Pawlett
Glyn Prawlett
Rose Davies
David James
Melbourne Williams
Clifford Brand
Ira Truelove
Christopher David
Tyron Duncan
?
Derek Gainfort
David Gainfort
?
?
Peter John
Kenny Richards
Derek Davies
?
Brian Thomas
June Hughes
?
Rosemary Fountain

??, Heather Johnson, ?, .Pam Davies, Pam Davies, Terry Duncan, Desmond Davies, Jean Edwards, Joy Griffiths, Diane Davies, Patricia Hughes, ?, Michael Davies,?

Work and Leisure

OCCUPATIONS

Most occupations in Dale have been connected to the land or the sea with coffinmaking, coal merchant, transport, building and brewing, to name a few, as sidelines. The Castle Estate provided work as did military bases bringing work of a service nature including additional custom for the local shops and pubs. These and other occupations have been referred to elsewhere in this book, eg clergy and teachers.

The village had other shops, etc in the past... milliner, dressmaker, tailor, draper and grocer, shoemaker/cobbler, lodging house keeper, laundress, ironmonger, police constable, spinner, blacksmith.

In 1881 John Reynolds of No 2 Chapel Cottages had his blacksmith's shop on the site of the Coronation Hall. ▶ Edwin Thomas, another blacksmith, lived in No 1 Chapel Cottages. James Jenkins and his son, John, were the black-smiths in the mid 1800s.

There were petrol pumps and a dairy run by Sid and Iris Brooks near the current Village Hall. Sid, at 72 years of age, and Iris retired in November 1988 after 35 years of delivering milk in Dale, also papers in the winter. Sid and Iris missed only one day over those years .... to attend their son Christopher's graduation from Pontypridd Polytechnic.

Morgan's shop, the first house on Dale Quay opposite the Yacht Club, is now a private home and remembered by many, Polly Morgan in particular. The houses date from the seventeenth/eighteenth century. It is said that you could buy anything in Polly Morgan's .... if you could find it! *"What a shop it was, the stock of decades piled ceiling high. The Morgans were a large family in Dale but they have disappeared."* It was the end of an era when Polly died in 1938. After the Morgans, rats enjoyed 'tenancy' of the shop. The premises are said to be haunted, doors being opened and shut. The appearance of an open door where no door existed prompted one group of holidaymakers to pack up and leave!! Another veritable 'Aladdin's cave', was the grocers/general store on South Street kept by Mary Ann and George Roch – Mrs Roch the Shop not Mrs Roch, Coldstream - on the site of the current Post Office. This business was run by the Spriggs family in 1841 until the 1880s, followed by the Lees family into the 1900s.

One very important member of the working community was the midwife/nurse. In 1841 the midwife, lived at Castle Beach. They got around the area on push bikes, on call at all times except on their one day off per month!

Nurse Williams came and, almost left, in 1914! In June 1914 the Hon. President, presented the First Annual Report of the Dale & District Nurses Association -

"Nurse Williams commenced work on Jan 17th 1914...

Her tact & skill have given universal satisfaction, and we regard with pleasure, the withdrawal of her resignation. A casual survey of her work should convince all who object to the institution of a Parochial Nurse, that her presence is essential to the welfare of our community; and that we shall fail in our duty to the District should we allow the movement, so well begun, to perish or languish."

FEES
The services of the Nurse are free in ordinary cases of illness to those who subscribe:-
Cottagers   per annum   2s
Tradespeople   "   "   5s
Farmers   "   "   7s 6d, 15s
Others   "   "   £1 1s

MATERNITY FEES
For attendance at the Confinement, and for 10 days afterwards, if required:-
Cottagers   7s 6d
Tradespeople   10s 6d
Farmers   15s, £1 1s

Nurse Annie Sarah Powell was a founder member of the Dale Women's Institute in 1922 whilst fulfiling her nursing duties here, found time in 1928 to marry Percy Young of Merryborough and is seen riding the motorbike below. Nurses could not stay in post after their marriage so Nurse Nash too left when she married George Davies. Then followed in the 1930s and 40s Nurse Stewart, Nurse Bertha Jones, Nurse Olwyn Davies and Nurse Elizabeth Powell – who was married, the rules having changed. Nurses Gosling and Lewis were two of the last.

1927: Nurse Annie Sarah Powell

An occupation linked to nursing was undertaker. Mr William Davies of Brunt topped up his farming and carpentry income by making coffins for Tom Newing of Milford, having worked for him in the past. Newing sometimes made the coffins at a cost of £3.10.0 in 1935 rising, owing to increased material costs, to £7.5.0 in 1937. Mr Davies bought materials needed for jobs at the Castle from P H Wilkins, Furnishing & General Ironmonger, Haverfordwest

1 knot sash cord	3/-
7 sash fasteners	8/2
11 squares of glass	19/6.

1891 British Census:
Hooks Farm
George Bevans aged 13 Cowboy
...with boots and stetson, riding the range above Dale...
Perhaps not!!!

The Post

The arrival of a Post Office in Dale in the late1840s could follow on from the introduction in 1840 of a standard one penny charge irrespective of distance, using the famous 'Penny Black' stamps. The Postmaster, Isaac Phillips, and his wife, Mary, Assistant Postmaster appear for the first time as such on the 1851 Census – in 1841 Isaac Phillips was a Male Servant at Dale Castle. The Post Office, now known as The Old Post House, overlooking Castle Way and the Meadow and owned by Dale Castle Estate, is a Grade II listed, late eighteenth century house "probably rebuilt on a much earlier core, shown by the large external chimney". Isaac Phillips was still Postmaster in 1891 at the age of 75 years. After he died his second wife, Jane, continued until the early 1910s when John and Mary Sturley set up at The Brig. Mr Phillips sold a variety of items including the Indian and Ceylon teas advertised below -

Mr and Mrs Sturley had The Post House, now Hotel, built in South Street in 1927 where Mrs Sturley was Postmistress until 1950. Several Postmasters followed until Mrs Gloria David ran the business at Eaton Lodge in the early 1990s. In 1993 the Post Office moved to 2 South Street, a Grade II eighteenth century house used as a shop since at least 1841.

Mr William Sturley was postman in the village from 1903 until he transferred to Haverfordwest in 1931, retiring in 1950 after 46 years service. Mr Laddie Sheppard and his brother, Charlie, were the postmen for 24 years after Mr Sturley; Laddie covered The Drift up to St Ann's Head and Charlie the Village to Crabhall. When they retired in the 1950s the village had a number of postmen; the post was then sorted in Haverfordwest and brought by van.

The first record of a postman for Dale was of Mr John Cosker in the late 1840s. In 1882 he received good conduct stripes and badge from the Postmaster General for 36 years service as a Letter Carrier from Milford Haven to Dale and back. Before marrying John lived with his parents on North Street – 1851 aged 25 years. A newspaper report and Mr Warren Davies's response to it of 30th May 1883 records that during Mr Cosker's service the first 14 years he walked an average of 20 miles a day three days a week, a total of 43,680 miles. The next 22 years with a 6 day service – walking and on mule – he covered 137,280 miles, a total of 180,960 miles!! *"With the exception of about a fortnight at two different periods through a fall from his horse in frosty weather and one and a half days sickness, he has not failed to perform his duty constantly and regularly."* He continued as a Rural Postman for another 12 years, with a pony and cart then two ponies and a small mail cart, adding many more miles. He lived to be 86 years, NB Alun the Post, our current postman.

These postmen are respected by the community and remembered for their long service. *Laddie Sheppard* ▶

A one year contract with T H Bryan dated 30th December 1918 for the collection of Mails and their conveyance by Horse-drawn Vehicles", mail carts drawn by one or more horses, between Milford Haven P O (7.40am) via Herbrandstone S O, St Ishmaels Cross Roads for S O, Philbeach Lane for Marloes S O and Dale S O (9.35am), returning in the afternoon *"every week day in every week"* not Sunday.

'WASPS' it all about ....?
As they so skilfully tended their vegetables, the two sisters were increasingly bothered by wasps who had built two nests in the banks dividing their gardens. A badger came to help them one night and dug out both. Badgers are partial to wasps nests, particularly the fat grubs. Their mouth and nose seem impervious to stings and their coats are impenetrable. Now the ladies, whose coats are not impenetrable weed in peace!!   *July 1984*

SERVICES

Dale has several springs or wells and these were used for hundreds of years. A piped water supply was installed by Mr Lloyd-Philipps for Dale Castle and the village using water from the Castle reservoir near Drift Hill. The pipes were not connected to the houses but there were several taps from which water had to be carried. One was behind Polly Morgan's, another in South Street and another at Townsend. In times of drought, water had to be brought in by carts. Mains water services were installed in the 1930s.

Main sewerage did not reach Dale until 1953. Before then there were individual or larger cesspits. From the houses near the sea, the waste went straight into the sea. A story is told of children putting face-cloths, etc down the lavatory and then rushing out to the sewer outfall to retrieve them!

Electricity came to the village in stages. Before the system was completed in 1953, oil lamps and stoves were used.

In 1931, village roads were tarmacked, many for the first time. The contractors slept in bell tents in the Meadow.

A bus service was started by Mr T Davies, Windmill Farm, in the 1920s. He used his coal lorry, which was washed out on a Saturday, benches put in and a tarpaulin cover to provide the roof. Everyone used to climb on board for the trip to Milford, particularly farmers' wives taking eggs and butter to market. It became known as the 'Butter Tub'! ▶

This was followed by a more regular bus service from Greens Motors in the 1930s.

VILLAGE HALL

The last hut of the World War 1 Military Hospital on the Meadow was used as the Village Hall from c.1920 until 1953. It sat at the current junction of the new road and South Street where the Henry Tudor stone is sited. The Old Hall was well used for socials, dances, films, family events, cricket teas, entertaining the troops during and after World War 2 and special events.

The Old Hall was the centre for the Coronation Day Celebrations in 1937

> *Friday night was cinema night; the children could hardly wait for school to end to get home and ready for a good cowboy, love story or thriller, 'parked' on tables, benches, chairs, the floor, wherever …the highlight of the week.*

Another Coronation in 1953 gave its name to the new Hall – The Coronation Hall – officially opened in October 1953. Funds to build the new Hall were raised by collections from the villagers, organisations, fetes and other events plus loans from local farmers and built by Seymour Reynolds, a local contractor. The grand opening was presided over by a former Vicar of Dale, The Rev S B Williams. "Light refreshments followed the ceremony and then, to a packed audience, the first concert was held in the Hall." A large Committee had been formed, Chairman Bertie Warlow, to manage the project at an initial cost of £2134:4:6 as at 31 March 1954. At that date the funds raised amounted to £1750:4:5. The Committee continued to raise funds to pay off loans and for improvements and additions. When used on Coronation Day, 2 June 1953, the Hall only had a concrete floor; the wooden block floor was laid before the Official Opening. The third annual fete in 1955 raised £150 toward a porch and more heating equipment.

Over the years the Coronation Hall has been used for many social occasions and events eg Silver Jubilee (1977), Silver Wedding of Mr & Mrs Hugh Lloyd-Philipps (4 Nov 1982), 500th Anniversary of Henry Tudor Landing (7 Aug 1985) and recently to enthusiastically welcome in the Year 2000 with a capacity crowd. It is also regularly used by the Village School, W.I., Church and other organisations for concerts and fund-raising events as well as for weekly short mat bowls and monthly whist sessions. Church, youth and school groups 'from away' have also enjoyed the facilities, sometimes sleeping over. The Hall is a designated Emergency and Refuge Centre. Hall Committee members in June 1953 were -

back: *John Barrett, Hugh Lloyd-Philipps, Clifford Brand, Alex Fountain, Seymour Reynolds, Bertie Warlow, Lt J Elven*
front: *Billy Jenkins, Mrs Susan Reynolds, Mrs Jenkins, Llew Williams, Clement Warlow, ? Hawkey, Gwyn James*
not in photograph: Mrs Lloyd-Philipps (Sen), Mrs Gladys Rind, Bunny Rind

DALE FAIR and CARNIVAL

"Dale Fair! What magic those two words conjured up years ago and what memories they still evoke in some of us oldies. This was held each year in our village on August 5th. Robertus-de-Vale was empowered by Royal Charter on December 5th 1293 to hold a fair each year at his Manor of Vale in Pembrokeshire.

The excitement and preparation commenced the day before when villagers went around the farmers collecting milk to make the renowned Dale Fair Pudding; some would add a slice or so of butter. A rich, rice pudding with plenty of dried fruit and spice, especially large raisins, was baked always <u>very slowly</u> in large earthenware bowls. Delicious! With a creamy topping and pale golden skin, all visitors would expect a helping of pudding on Fair Day. Fair morning would see friends and relatives arriving mostly on foot or by boat, also the stallholders with fruit, sweets, ice cream and chip carts (both horse drawn) from Haverfordwest. The fairground people arrived the previous day to set up along the beach road watched by most of the village children dancing around with excitement.

Children's sports were on the meadow in the afternoon; later the whole village joined in. Everyone was dressed in their best .... no lady was properly dressed without her hat and gloves. Just imagine the ladies taking part in a sack or wheelbarrow race wearing their large, flower and feather bedecked hats!

Dale Fair c1920s ▶

One not so pleasant memory was of 'the teasers', small, metal tubes filled with water!! These were purchased mostly by the lads to squirt the ladies who didn't take this meekly, striking them around the ears with sawdust balls on elastic .... the shrieks could be heard far afield!! As they wended their way home all agreed that it had been another good Dale Fair."

Marjorie Johnson (nee Sturley) re late 1920s.

THE HAVERFORDWEST
& MILFORD HAVEN
TELEGRAPH
August 17th 1898
The annual Fair and Sports was was held on the 5th inst although the weather was wet and windy, there were present a fairly large assemblage of pleasure seekers. A programme was drawn up of children and adult flat races, wheeling a barrow blind-folded, throwing a weight, tug of war, running in socks, rowing matches and smoking tobacco.

Winners were listed but not for 'smoking tobacco'!!

Sadly interest waned in the 1940s and the Fair came to an end. Although there had been similar events in the village after World War 2, *"Blazing sunshine attracted hundreds of local people and holiday makers to the first annual Dale Carnival and Sports"* and was reported in the press in July 1969 as *"one of the most successful events in the seaside village for a number of years"*. Organised by a Committee to celebrate the Investiture of the Prince of Wales, a pattern was set for years to come.

'Dale Auxiliary Fire Team' c1987

Floats and walking entries were judged and the first fairy princess, Cheryl Klass, crowned before parading through the village. In later years a carnival queen was crowned attended by the fairy princess.

Stalls and sideshows set up in the meadow attracted those attending, with displays by the Swansea Marching Band, West Side All Stars Comedy Band from Swansea in 1982 when rain lashed the Carnival, the Coastguard Rescue Team and RAF Sea King of 202 Squadron and the Haverfordwest Town and County Band in 1983. As at Dale Fair sports for the young and not-so-young were organised.

Dale Carnival came to an end in the late 1980s, its passing regretted by many in the village.

STORMY WEATHER

The oft expressed view that the sun always shines on Dale is not strictly true but we certainly seem to have our fair share and more. Forecast maps on television invariably have a 'sun symbol' over the Dale Peninsula; in 1965 it was recorded that Dale was the sunniest place in England, Scotland and Wales with 1,793.5hrs of sunshine. However, over the years there have been a number of spectacular, even awesome, storms resulting in numerous shipwrecks – see previous chapters. Dale Meadow has been flooded on a number of occasions following high tides, 1937 and 1988. Opening Day of the Car Park in May 1993 saw the car park under water! Also the sea wall by Eaton Hall and The Griffin Inn has been breached several times, the last being in December 1989. The Griffin and other properties required the services of the Fire Brigade to pump out water on these occasions also when a Spring or Autumn High Tide rises up over the wall in dramatic style. In 1936 it was the sea wall and road by Brook House and Brook Cottage that was washed away; for several months traffic could only reach the village via Castle Way. Those who live by the sea have a healthy respect for its power.

1937: Dale Meadow flooded after a high tide

Easter 1985: High tide

Our position and climate often mean we escape snow... there can be snow in Milford or Haverfordwest but not in Dale! As with the rest of the country, Dale was affected by the severe snow storms of 1947. However, the Force 10 blizzard which hit Pembrokeshire in February 1978 completely paralysed traffic movement in, out and around Dale for nearly a week. Cars were 'lost' in 10 feet drifts and villagers found themselves walking on top of vehicles on their way to collect milk, etc at local farms. All telephone cables were down and no mobile 'phones! Emergency supplies of baby milk powder and foods and medicines were brought in by helicopter, other supplies arriving by boat. Bread and other rations were collected from the beach. Most were without electricity; as there is no mains gas in the village, cooking became a matter for ingenuity and co-operation. Those with Raeburns, Agas, etc offered help with boiling water and cooking. Community spirit was high despite the hardships and fears. As most were unable to go to work out of the village a bit of a holiday and party atmosphere developed.

YACHTING ADVENTURES

1965: Campbell Reynold's nephew Brian Thomas, then aged 23, sailed from Lymington with the legendary mountaineer and explorer Major Bill Tilman. In his ex-Bristol Channel cutter, MISCHIEF, this spartan, 4 month expedition – with no lifesaving equipment, radio, etc and just a sextant and chronometer – was an attempt to navigate through the ice-bound coast of East Greenland. The expedition was successful and enabled Tilman, then aged 65, to land, climb and leave before the winter ice closed in.

1971: Nicolette Milnes-Walker set off from Dale to become the first woman to make a non-stop, single-handed voyage across the Atlantic, covering 3,500 miles in just 6 weeks. Her 30ft sloop, AZIZ, was fitted out by Dale craftsmen and she flew the Dale Yacht Club burgee. She presented this to the Club on her return and it can still be seen there. In Newport, Rhode Island, Nicky asked for *"a bath, a large steak and a long sleep"*. ▶

1991: Campbell Reynolds realised his life long ambition to sail the Atlantic. He, together with Professor Bunning and Richard Gau, visited the West Indies in the 38ft Rival ORBIT and then sailed back again, covering 8,300 nautical miles. After leaving Dale on 26th September they sailed via Madeira, Gran Canaria, Barbados and up through St Vincent to Martinique. Campell's log entry in St Lucia - *"Monday 13th Jan '92 : Walked into a Bar in Castries and sat at adjoining table to lady & gent.. I thought I recognised them... I said to the wife – who comes from Dale then? Jeremy David turned around complete with DYC jumper! Unbelievable!"* They completed the 6 months round trip on 2nd March 1992.

YACHT CLUB

The Dale Regatta dates back to the 1920s. A committee, which held its meetings at The Griffin, organised this annual event. The 'Stella Maris' Cup was one of the trophies competed for as well as money prizes. Dinghies were towed or sailed from neighbouring yachting places. During World War 2 the Regatta was suspended but afterwards, with help from RNAS Kete, re-formed. The Dale Nursery Co lorry acted as Race Control and used to transport the dinghies and their owners during the post war petrol shortage.

Plans were made to start a Yacht Club, sailing G P Dinghies, in many cases owner-built from wooden kits. Weekly races began and in 1958 there was a regular turnout of at least 18 boats. The next year the present premises, formerly a warehouse, were bought and members worked hard to convert the building. Fortuitiously, some large timber planks were washed up on Dale beach and promptly salvaged! The Club was extended and showers put in. Social functions were held as well as sailing meetings, one of the most popular being the Sunday lunchtime opening of the bar when pubs in Pembrokeshire were 'dry'. A cruiser racing weekend was started in the 1970s with visiting boats from other parts of Wales, England and Ireland.

◄ *Dale Regatta: 1940s*

FUN AND FAME

Over the years the village has enjoyed many a celebration, details of which have been related elsewhere. Coronation Days (1911 and 1937), Golden and Silver Jubilees (1935 and 1977), Empire Days, as well as events such as Balloon Racing in 1936, are all well documented and remembered.

Since the war, leisure boating has increased enormously and moorings have been regulated since the early 1980s. There is much 'pottering about' with boats of all shapes and sizes, in and out of the water. Divers have used Dale as a base for visiting local wrecks, etc since about 1970 and windsurfers have been coming since 1984. Boating trips have also proved popular with the EMPRESS in the 1960s, an ex-lifeboat the DALE QUEEN in the 1970s, an ex-army DUKW being used to ferry pasengers from the beach to the DALE QUEEN, fishing trips in the 1980s in the GIULIANA III and since 1980 the DALE PRINCESS.

One nationally acclaimed event for television, 'Sea of Galilee', saw Jimmy Sturley, Jock Ramsay, John Sturley and George Sturley don unfamiliar, period costume to act their part in the making of this film. The sea, however, was more familiar territory to the Sturleys as local fisherman than their role as disciples!

PUBS, CLUBS and ORGANISATIONS

According to popular tradition, there were 18 pubs in Dale at one time. Some of them can be traced back through written records. These probably catered for visiting sailors as well as locals.

In 1705 there was a reference to the Brewhouse so there may have been an inn to go with it, although a lot of Dale's ale was exported by boat.

In the Archeological Survey of c1900 there is mention of the remains of a building, formerly a public house, where – probably about 1780 – several loose women had resided. Even worse, some Portugese sailors who visited the place were never seen again and it was suspected they had been murdered. Later, in about 1870, soldiers from Dale Fort found a cache of silver coins, said to have been foreign dollars, hidden under the plaster of what remained of the walls. They sold the coins to Ben Lyon the Jew in Pembroke Dock. This information was given to Mr Mathias, compiler of the Survey, by the Serjeant in Charge after the soldiers had left the Fort. There is another report (only hearsay) that a public house was situated alongside the Point Road. A building called the Cupola existed there around 1790 which was reputedly the haunt of smugglers.

Schedule (A).

FORM OF RECOGNIZANCE.

Pembrokeshire.} AT a General Meeting of His Majesty's Justices of the Peace (to wit.) acting in and for the Hundred of _Roose_ in the said County, held at _Haverfordwest_ on _Saturday_ the _Twenty fourth_ of September, One Thousand Eight Hundred and Twenty _five_ _Thomas Morgans_ at the Sign of the _Skips_ in the Parish of _Dale_ Victualler, acknowledges himself to be indebted to our Sovereign Lord the King, in the Sum of Thirty Pounds, and _John Roberts_ of the Parish of _Marloes_ acknowledges himself to be indebted to our Sovereign Lord the King in the Sum of Twenty Pounds, to be levied upon their several Goods and Chattels, Lands and Tenements, by way of Recognizance to His Majesty's Use, His Heirs and Successors, upon Condition that the said _Thomas Morgans_ do and shall keep the true Assize in uttering and selling Bread and other Victuals, Beer, Ale, and other Liquors in his, ~~her or their~~ House, and shall not fraudulently dilute or adulterate the same, and shall not use, in uttering and selling thereof, any Pots or other Measures that are not of full Size, and shall not wilfully or knowingly permit Drunkenness or Tippling, nor get drunk in his, ~~her or their~~ House or other Premises; nor knowingly suffer any gaming with Cards, Draughts, Dice, Bagatelle, or any other sedentary Game, in his, ~~her or their~~ House, or any of the Outhouses, Appurtenances, or Easements thereto belonging, by Journeymen, Labourers, Servants, or Apprentices; nor knowingly introduce, permit, or suffer any Bull, Bear, or Badger-baiting, Cock-fighting, or other such Sport or Amusement in any Part of his, ~~her or their~~ Premises; nor shall knowingly or designedly, and with a View to harbour and entertain such, permit or suffer Men or Women of notoriously bad Fame, or dissolute Girls and Boys to assemble and meet together in his, ~~her or their~~ House, or any of the Premises thereto belonging; nor shall keep open his, ~~her or their~~ House, nor permit or suffer any drinking or tippling in any Part of his, ~~her or their~~ Premises during the usual Hours of Divine Service on Sundays; nor shall keep open his, ~~her or their~~ House or other Premises during late Hours of the Night, or early in the Morning, for any other Purpose than the Reception of Travellers, but do keep good Rule and Order therein according to the Purport of a Licence granted for selling Ale, Beer, or other Liquors by Retail in the said House and Premises for One whole Year, commencing on the Tenth Day of October next, then this Recognizance to be void, or else to remain in full force.

In 1795, three persons in Dale were licensed to keep alehouses. One of them was The Ship, now known as The Brig and no longer a pub, on Dale Quay. The building was erected in 1750 by Robert Mussevin a Dutchman – some reports think he may have been Norwegian. It was occupied by Lewis Sanderson and he is one of the named alehouse licence-holders in 1795. In 1822 it was named as The Ship and this may have been the name since its foundation. During the next few years the landlords changed several times and the name also changed to The Royal William in 1834 and The Brig by 1873. It may have ended its life as a pub in 1922 when the lease to the brewer, James Williams, Narberth, ran out.

Another pub was possibly The Blue Anchor sited above the present Blue Anchor Way. In the 1841 Census a lady named Dinah Geary, whose address was Dale Cliff, was an innkeeper by profession. Tradition has it that this may have been The Drum and Monkey. The Three Horseshoes, landlord Thomas Morgans, was given a licence in 1822. By 1824 the landlord was William Thomas and the name had changed to The Griffin. This is the one remaining pub in Dale.

◀ *Mr George Bernard White, landlord of The Three Horseshoes/The Griffin, is pictured on the left with his wife and their pet dog.*
Mr White died aged 42 years in 1915.

CLUBS and ORGANISATIONS

Over the years there has been a variety of clubs and organisations in Dale for boys and girls, men and women. Photographs show The Girl Guides in the late 1920s and Girls' Friendly Society c1915, led by Miss Penruddock and The Rev SB and Mrs Williams respectively. For the boys in the late 1930s a Sea Scout group of six members plus Cyril Thomas as Leader was formed, uniforms having been provided by Colonel Lloyd-Phillips; although the emphasis was on outdoor activities they sometimes met in the Reading Room, South Street, or in the W.I. Hut on Castle Way. In 1941 it was reported that the Hut had suffered *"some damage by the Scouts"*! The W.I. Hut was also being used in the early 1940s by the Girl Guides and the Girls' Friendly Society …no reports of damage. Dale Boys' Club was established, subs to be paid to Tony Fisher, complete with Rules *1. Club Members only to use the room, 2. No one under 15 years to be a member, 3. Subscription 3/- a month, 4. Club Room to be kept clean, 5. No noise – shouting – banging of doors because of nuisance to neighbours, 6. Club closed on Sundays, 7. Any damage to be made good.*

In 1924 Miss Dale of Dale seemed to be a star of the Tennis Club…

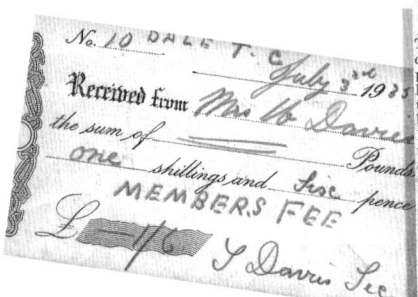

LAWN TENNIS TOURNAMENT.

On Wednesday, the 5th inst., the Dale Lawn Tennis team visited Marloes, where a very exciting and sporting tournament was held. Dale players played well, and are to be congratulated on their splendid victory. The game of the evening was the ladies' "singles," played between Mrs. Rowlands, Marloes, and Miss Dale, of Dale. These ladies played very hard throughout their game, and gave a very fine exposition of the game. The following is a list of the games :—
Ladies' Singles.—Miss Dale (Dale) beat Mrs. Rowlands (Marloes) 8—6.
Gentlemen's Singles.—Mr. Keen (Dale) beat Mr. Rowlands (Marloes) 6—1.
Gentlemen's Doubles.—Mr. Rowlands and Mr. Hayden (Marloes) beat Mr. Fisher and Mr. Roberts (Dale) 6—2.
Ladies' Doubles.—Miss Johns and Miss E. Allen (Dale) beat Mrs. Devonald and Nurse Hagstrom 6—1.

…whilst the Dale Cricket Team went by boat to play at Angle. Matches between the Marloes and Dale Clubs were often full of incidents –

One day a Marloes man was bowling to Willie Howells, Dale. The ball hit Willie on the ankle. Umpire shouted "Not out". Same happened a second and a third time. Then the umpire called Willie over and said "Willie, if he hits you there again, I'll have to give you out"!
The Umpire was Willie Reynolds from Dale.

Whist is an activity which has stood the test of time in Dale as has the Womens' Institute (W I).

1922-23

Dale W I was set up in 1922, a branch of the infant, nationwide movement aiming to develop and improve rural life, to promote the fuller education of countrywomen, also international understanding. It was a non-political and non-religious movement. Some of the founder members in Dale were Nurse Bottin, Mrs M E Lloyd-Philipps, Nurse Powell and Mrs G Rind. Meetings took place monthly, often at Allenbrook, until the W I Hut was erected in 1937. We now meet twice-monthly.

Members interests were, as today, raised and ranged from cookery demonstrations – faggots and chips in 1939 – courses in craftwork such as dressmaking, basketry and patchwork proving popular as well as lecturers on first aid, even in 1938 'A Women's Influence in the Home'. They also took part in county and nationwide events, some members visiting the W I's own Education Centre, Denman College – one lady came back to report that it was a really worthwhile visit and no-one need be afraid of going!

During the war members worked hard for the war effort, picking fruit such as sloes and making jam – bread and jam being a staple part of everyone's diet during the war – collecting for the Red Cross, sewing for the hospitals, collecting 'salvage' and planting extra vegetables. They also operated a canning machine. Whist drives, dances etc were organised for the troops stationed here.

Dale W I has always made a contribution to community affairs .... Christmas parties for the children for over 50 years, gifts to patients in Kensington Hospital, fundraising for the Coronation Hall, a Youth Club in the 1970s, annual litter collections and refreshments laid on for village events, etc. Following the Re-enactment in 1985 of the Henry Tudor landing, Dale W I created a wall-hanging of this historic event, using different mediums.

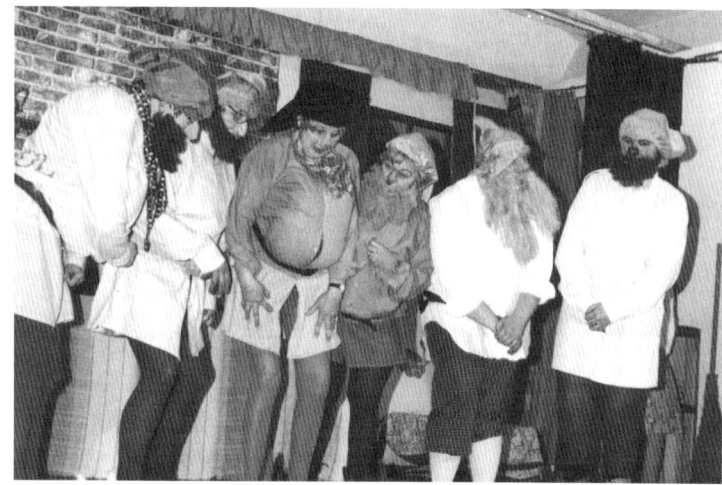

Where's the seventh dwarf?

The W I has also raised money and materials for many needy causes. Following discussions, letters have been written requesting improvements in village amenities and on national and international issues such as G M foods and the preservation of the village post office. Much amusement, often unintentionally, has been provided as members 'tripped the light fantastic' in many dramatic and other productions. Rehearsals frequently dissolved in laughter when a stray foot separated costume from wearer, false noses applied or just 'a look' exchanged! Members have enjoyed quizzes, treasure hunts and 'letting their hair down' with at times humorous consequences; unaccustomed to a celebratory beverage one member was searching the next day for her car ... by which time she had removed the pickled onions from her eyes! We are always open to widening our horizons ... pity the 'alternative calendar' has been 'done'!!

FINAL THOUGHTS

In the year of the Millennium,
Before it was too late,
The W I had a notion
To commemorate that date.

We put it to the meeting
And the decision that they took
Was to find out all the data
To write a Village Book.

We put our heads together
To form a Project Group.
Application to the Lottery
And some money we did scoop.

With great enthusiasm
We set about the task.
To gather information,
All the village we did ask.

They rummaged in their attics
And amazing things did find,
Like photographs and cuttings
Their folk had left behind.

We delve into the records
And any books we can,
To find out all the history
To help us with our plan.

With a wealth of information
From time to time we met
To report back to the editors;
A deadline has been set.

We've got it all together ...
Computerized at last!!
An interesting reflection
Of happenings in the past.

We've passed it to the printer,
Text, pictures large and small,
Ready to be published ...
A relief to one and all!

It has been hard work and taken up much leisure time but we have gained enormously through researching and writing this book. We hope Dale folk today will be as diligent as their ancestors have been in hoarding photographs, newspaper cuttings, information and anecdotes to enable someone/a group to update this book in the future.

SELECT SOURCES AND BIBLIOGRAPHY

Arch Cam 1915, 1919
'Archaeological Survey (Pembs) Report of 1896-1907'
'Cambrian Register' 1795
'Dale Congregational Chapel Sunday School Register'
'Dale Parish Church Records'
'Great Castle Head, Dale, Archaeological Excavation and Survey' 1999 Archaeoleg Cambria Archaeology/Cadw: Welsh Historic Monuments
'HM Coastguards and MCA Log Books and Records'
'Survey of Ancient Monuments Report' (Pembs) 1920
'The Journal of the Pembrokeshire Historial Society No 3' 1989
'Three books of English History' Polydore Vergil 1844
'Welsh Historic Monuments: Statutory List for Dale' Cadw
'British Census 1841, 1851, 1861, 1871, 1881, 1891'
'Tithe Map and Schedule of Dale 1847'
'1814 Map'
BARRETT, John 'A Plain Man's Guide to the Dale Peninsula' 1966, 1981, plus unpublished material
CHARLES, B G 'The Placenames of Pembrokeshire 1992
DRESSER, Barbara 'Land Use & Farm Practice in the Parish of Dale
EDWARDS, J Dudley 'Dale & St Brides – Some of Their History' c1975, plus unpublished material
FENTON 'Historical Tour Through Pembrokeshire' 1810
GEORGE, Barbara 'Pembrokeshire Sea Trading before 1900' 1964
LEWIS 'Topographical Dictionary of Wales' 1833
LEWIS, E A 'Welsh Port Books' 1927
HASLAM, Charlotte 'West Blockhouse' Landmark Trust 1990
HUCKETT, The Rev Andrew W 'HMS Harrier at Kete'
MORRELL, Stephen L 'A Short History of Dale Fort' 1999
MORRIS, Lewis 'Survey of Maritime History' 1748
OWEN, G 'Description of Pembrokeshire' 1596
OWEN, H ' Old Pembrokeshire Families' 1902
RAWLINGS, Bert J 'The Parish Churches & Nonconfirmist Chapels of Wales Vol 1'
THOMAS, Roger 'West Blockhouse Fort 1939-45' and 'Survey of 19th & 20th C Military Buildings of Pembrokeshire'
TRUELOVE, S 'Extracts from Dale School Log'
WHEELER, N J 'The Fortification of Milford Haven & Pembroke Dock' Pembs Coast National Park
WHITE, George 'Tramlines to the Stars: George White of Bristol' 1995
Select references from Malcolm CULLEN, John EVANS, Brigr GOUGH, David NORGATE, Roland THORNE
Select newspaper cuttings – The Haverfordwest & Milford HavenTelegraph

Archaeoleg Cambria   )
Haverfordwest Reference Library   )   with grateful thanks to the Staff for their help
Pembrokeshire Records Office   )   in finding relevant references
Tenby Museum   )